DELINQUENTS AND CRIMINALS: THEIR SOCIAL WORLD

HOLBROOK PRESS SOCIOLOGY SERIES
Readings in Sociology

HOLBROOK PRESS, INC.
Boston

DELINQUENTS AND CRIMINALS: THEIR SOCIAL WORLD

Compiled and edited by
Helen MacGill Hughes, Ph.D.

Sociological Resources for the Social Studies
SPONSORED BY THE
AMERICAN SOCIOLOGICAL ASSOCIATION
SUPPORTED BY THE
NATIONAL SCIENCE FOUNDATION

Printed in the United States of America
Library of Congress Catalog Card Number 70–128906

Foreword

The "what is" of the social world is of primary interest to the sociologist. He wants to know about existing patterns of human relationships, why they are as they are (their causes), and what consequences they have for people, groups, and society in general (their effects). But to find out what, in fact, these patterns of relationship are, the sociologist must study society itself. He must conduct research on group behavior, studying how various groups are related to one another and to the institutions of society.

Take, for example, the militant political groups of young people that sprang up in the late sixties. The sociologist tries to understand the conditions and events in society generally and the experiences in family, school, and peer groups that have led the members of these groups to organize and establish their programs of activities. He also seeks to discover the effects of such activities on universities, communities, and political life in the whole society. Thus his research into a particular kind of group adds to knowledge about other groups and institutions and how they function in society.

Because research plays such a major role in learning about our society, it is important that various research studies on a particular topic be brought together in one place so that we may have a more comprehensive picture of that topic. *Racial and Ethnic Relations* is a book of such research studies. It is made up of a set of readings that present in clear language the results of important sociological research. Studies on which the readings are based were done by competent social scientists, and each volume in this *Readings in Sociology* Series therefore presents significant information in its field.

The selections included in each volume not only present research results but also reveal the methods used by investigators to obtain those results. By studying these volumes, students can learn what social scientists do and how they do it.

Many distinguished sociologists have worked in collaboration with instructors in designing and writing materials for the project. The central staff has seen these materials through the long process of national trial, evaluation, and revision.

The SRSS materials are suitable for use in a variety of social science courses where they can enhance the existing curriculum by adding a sociological perspective. For example, in addition to use in sociology courses, the materials may be easily integrated into such courses as history, social problems, economics, and political science. In addition, some materials are well suited for such courses as English, mathematics, psychology, family life, and the humanities.

The aim of the SRSS project has been to provide materials which are relevant to the interests and concerns of students and which afford them an understanding of sociological concepts and methods at work.

Robert C. Angell

Preface

We are living in a time when delinquency and crime are taking new forms. Many crimes, such as the buying or selling of "pot" or heroin, are being committed by very youthful offenders. This development, which began in the 1950s, has given rise to new problems in law enforcement and rehabilitation. At the same time, serious adult crime seems to be on the increase in many American cities. The phrase "crime in the streets" has a powerful political impact, but like another phrase, "law and order," it has become part of the language of public business only within the last few years.

Delinquency used always to be spoken of as *juvenile delinquency*. That meant it referred to violations of the law by young offenders. It still does, but today we usually drop the word *juvenile*. Crime is the word used to mean violations of the law by adults. There is a third term, deviance. In recent years sociologists have been using the word deviance to mean behavior which may not be, in itself, illegal, but which is a departure from normal behavior and which is very likely to involve lawbreaking. Thus drunkenness is not against the law, but one may be arrested for being drunk in a public place. And it is not illegal to be "high" on "pot" or other drugs, but to obtain marijuana the drug user must make connections with the underworld, and if he owns, or buys, or sells any narcotic drug, he becomes guilty of a very serious offense.

Most of the readings in this book are on the subject of delinquency, and only a few deal with crime. *Each was chosen because it reports some interesting sociological discovery. Thus these selections may be read in any order at all; they are not intended to build up a systematic theory of offenders and their offenses. But they each report something that sociologists have learned about one of our most pressing and distressing problems.*

The first selection discusses the sociologists' view of delinquency, crime, and deviance and the methods used by the authors of the nineteen pieces of research which are described in the remainder of the book.

Selections two, three, and four analyze delinquent behavior: what it is, how much delinquency there is in the United States, and how a young person becomes officially delinquent. There follows—in selection five—a description of the choices of behavior available to a young person—at home and at school—*before* he or she actually commits an offense.

Selections six and seven follow the boy or girl into actual delinquency, showing, in particular, what may follow if the family or neighborhood fails to give moral support and good examples. In selection eight, delinquents are classed by the social status of the schools they attend. Especially interesting are the findings in cases where the status of the school and the status of the youth's family do not match.

The ninth selection describes the particular nature of delinquent behavior among middle-class youth. Here it is clearly shown that poverty and deprivation do not explain the offender— for young people who are given (or who succeed in earning) good cars and ample pocket money also get into trouble with the law. Selection ten is adapted from one of the classic essays in criminology: Professor Edwin Sutherland's article on business crime. Most business crime is committed by members of the middle class and often it is not recognized as crime at all. Thus in these two selections middle-class delinquency and middle-class crime are distinguished from the corresponding behavior in the working class.

In selections eleven and twelve, the delinquent youth as a person—rather than delinquent behavior—is the center of interest. The young boy or girl whose offense is shoplifting or other forms of theft is distinguished from the boy (it is almost never a girl) who steals cars. And in the thirteenth piece, the family of the recidivist (the "repeater") is shown as a powerful influence upon whether or not its kinsman will "go straight" on being released from training school or prison.

The fourteenth selection considers the fascinating subject of crime "waves." The article which surveys Boston for a period of over a century depicts crime as undergoing a succession of increases and decreases. The troughs and peaks accompany wars, depressions, inflation, and other epochs and events in society at large and Boston in particular; but the author does not claim that these things *cause* crime waves. With the fifteenth selection, the case of Puerto Rico is used to show how lawlessness makes its appearance when a simpler society develops cities and industries. Attention then turns—in selection sixteen—to crimes that are committed on a large scale and that require the organized effort of many "specialists." Like all crime, organized crime can thrive best where there is not strong opposition to it. Thus in selection seventeen the public's attitude towards two forms of organized crime—graft and gambling—is described, and it is shown that in a certain eastern city gambling was looked on more tolerantly than was graft.

The book concludes with a consideration of deviant behavior, much of which is socially condemned, though not illegal. This theme was actually introduced in the selection just mentioned, since gambling, for example, is illegal only in certain forms. In a sense this may also be said of violence. Political protest by demonstration, parading, picketing, and the like is acceptable under a democratic government. The "traitors to the King," of 1776 were patriotic heroes to the citizens of the Thirteen Colonies —except to those in the Tory minority. But if the political protest should include bodily injury, looting, and the destruction of property—sometimes the mere act of meeting together on the streets—it passes on into illegal behavior. Selection eighteen offers an analysis of the role of rioting in American history and in the present, of the conditions under which riots occur, and of those who take part in them.

The article on Skid Row—selection nineteen—pictures the existence (very often in its final stages) of men whose lives have been ruined by heavy drinking. It shows that even so disorganized and rejected a company as a group of drunken vagrants follows rites and rules of its own making and builds a society of its own. The final selection reports the facts about the use of alcohol and drugs and something of what is known of their connection with delinquency and crime. It is impossible to get reliable statistics, for the traffic in drugs is carried on in secret, underground, and the available figures account for only the small fraction which is discovered. On this subject, social scientists must, to some degree, work in the dark.

The questions which precede each selection are questions which the author of the research hoped to answer by his studies. They are not intended as questions to be put to the student. It will be noticed that in some articles the statistics are of a later date than the research itself. In such cases the author or the rewriter has undertaken to bring the facts up-to-date for this book.

At the end of the book is a list of selected readings, keyed by number to the selections on which they have a bearing.

Sociological Resources for the Social Studies gratefully acknowledges advice and suggestions for this book from the following scholars: Ruth Shonle Cavan, Marshall B. Clinard, Earl Rubington, Negley Teeters, Jackson Toby, and Stanton Wheeler.

It also gratefully acknowledges permission kindly given by the following publications and publishers to adapt selections for this book: *The American Journal of Psychiatry, The American Journal of Sociology, American Sociological Review, The Annals of the American Academy of Political and Social Science, The Canadian Journal of Economics and Political Science, Federal Probation,* Free Press, *The Journal of Criminal Law, Criminology, and Police Science, The Journal of Social Issues, Quarterly Journal of Studies on Alcohol, Social Change and Public Policy, Social Forces, Social Problems, Sociological Inquiry, The Sociological Quarterly.*

It acknowledges, too, the services of the following writers who adapted the selections: Warren Breed, James Cornell, Eleanor Gates, Sally Martin, Norman Ritter, Stanley Schuler, and the editorial services of Nancy Stein Seasholes.

Contents

	Foreword	v
	Preface	vii
1.	Sociologists Look at Delinquency and Crime *by Thorsten Sellin*	1
2.	What Is Delinquent Behavior? *from Ruth S. Cavan*	9
3.	Who Is a Delinquent and Who Is Not? *from Irving Piliavin and Scott Briar*	18
4.	How Much Delinquency Is There? *from Maynard L. Erickson and LaMar T. Empey*	27
5.	The Candidate for Delinquency *from Larry Karacki and Jackson Toby*	43
6.	The Slum: Opportunities for Crime and Delinquency *from Richard A. Cloward and Lloyd E. Ohlin*	51
7.	Lower-Class Culture and Delinquency *from Walter B. Miller*	62
8.	Delinquency and Social Status *from Albert J. Reiss, Jr. and Albert Lewis Rhodes*	72
9.	Middle-Class Delinquency *from Joseph W. Scott and Edmund W. Vaz*	80
10.	White-Collar Criminality *from Edwin H. Sutherland*	91
11.	Teen-Agers Who Steal *from Robert A. Dentler and Lawrence J. Monroe*	102
12.	Stealing Cars *from Erwin Schepses*	112
13.	Cell 202: Who Will Come Back? *from Harold Finestone*	120
14.	Crime Waves: The Record of 120 Years in Boston *from Theodore N. Ferdinand*	128

15.   Crime and Newcomers to the City
                        from Marshall B. Clinard   142

16.   Organized Crime and Its Social Effects
                        from Earl Johnson, Jr.   149

17.   Graft, Gambling, and Public Opinion
                        from John A. Gardiner   157

18.   Riots: Past and Present Violence
                        from John P. Spiegel   165

19.   Life on Skid Row
         from Samuel E. Wallace; also Earl Rubington   175

20.   Drugs and Drug Users
                        from Richard A. Blum   186

       Suggested Reading   196

       Index   205

Sociologists Look at
Delinquency and Crime*

In the periodic surveys of American public opinion since World War II, crime has gradually moved to the top in the ranking of our most pressing social problems. Alarm has been nourished by the statistical reports of the Federal Bureau of Investigation (the FBI) and the police departments of our big cities, all of which show that the rates of serious criminality have been rising steadily in recent years. The publicity given to such information by the mass media, the unending stream of newspaper reports of murders, rapes, robberies, muggings, vandalism, and riots, with accounts given by the victims of their personal experiences, have aroused the public.

Demands for drastic remedial action, for "law and order," for "safe streets," or for "getting tough" with lawbreakers have become more and more insistent. Congressional committees have printed thousands of pages of hearings on juvenile delinquency and organized crime, state commissions have been set up to study the matter and propose solutions, and within the last two years two important national commissions have issued voluminous reports with hundreds of recommendations on how to cope with it by improving our system of criminal justice and by taking preventive social action.

But if it is to strike at the roots of crime, preventive social action must rest on an understanding of the causes of crime. To provide an explanation of crime is the still unfinished work of the social scientists, in particular sociologists, psychologists, and psychiatrists. They study the conduct of persons by various means and from various points of view. Sociologists mainly look on a person as the product of the social groups to which he belongs. They are, therefore, interested in knowing the characteristics of groups, the rules or norms by which they influence the conduct of their members, and the nature of that influence, considering

---

* Written for this book by Thorsten Sellin, University of Pennsylvania.

that members are not all alike in their capacity to adapt themselves to the demands and pressures of group life. Many of the articles in this book illustrate this approach to the study of delinquency; for example the selections on gangs and their family and neighborhood backgrounds.

Many people think of crime as serious attacks on persons or property, for these are the events that are featured in our newspapers. Actually, however, crime is any act which the criminal law defines and threatens with punishment by fine, imprisonment, or perhaps death, depending on the importance a legislature attaches to the injury caused to persons, their property, or the community at large. Disorderly conduct and murder are both crimes at law, although the first is a minor offense and the second is a major crime and the two are at opposite poles on the scale of punishments.

"Crime" and "delinquency" are legal terms. "Deviance"—a third term which has recently come into common use—is not a legal term. In the articles in this book, the sociologists who use the term deviance assume the existence of norms or rules of conduct which a social group expects its members to obey, within certain limits of tolerance. Conduct which departs from this average in excess or not enough would then be considered deviant whether it is illegal or not. Ruth S. Cavan's article deals in part with this problem.

Since 1899, when juvenile courts came into being, delinquency has denoted offenses which would be crimes if committed by adults, that is, persons above a certain age, usually 18 years. In nearly all states (New York is one exception) delinquency also includes some conduct not punishable if committed by adults, such as truancy, incorrigibility, and running away from home. The definition of delinquency was created both to permit courts to apply to juveniles procedures different from those used in criminal cases and to permit more flexible means of treatment than those applicable to adults.

Some sociologists are interested in the effect of the correctional system, of social crises, and of population changes and movements on crime rates, and have included the study of political and economic institutions and some special cultural characteristics which influence the conduct of individuals. One such study is the work of Marshall B. Clinard, who selected Puerto Rico as his place of study and sought to find what it is in city life that so often turns a peaceable peasant into a disorderly townsman. The fact that cities have higher rates of crime than small towns and rural districts is well known. But city life is new to thousands in Puerto Rico, and seeing the drama of increasing urbanization and increasing crime, as played out there today, is like seeing a re-play of what happened decades ago as the population of mainland cities grew.

Theodore N. Ferdinand uses the number of persons arrested for various serious offenses to establish crude rates which are assumed to show the changes in criminality during the period studied and to permit certain conclusions about the major reasons why the rates fluctuate—for instance, the effect of the economic cycle, war, the automobile, migration, population growth, and immigration.

It is obviously important to know whether criminality and delinquency are increasing or decreasing in a given community or area or in a given class of persons. We need such measures or indexes in order to test the effectiveness of preventive social action, for one thing, as well as to learn the kind of correlations made by Ferdinand.

It is now generally recognized, however, that only a few types of crime recorded by the police can provide reasonably accurate indications of trends. It is assumed that the known fraction of such criminality remains constant from year to year in relation to the portion that escapes police notice for one reason or another.

Other types of crime brought to the attention of the police—apart from the seven major offenses—cannot provide reliable indexes to real criminality. This may be because the number of crimes recorded depends on how active are the police patrols, or is too small because the crimes are very difficult to discover (as are most sex offenses, political corruption, bribery, and the traffic in narcotic drugs).

It is possible to gather official information about offenders, evident or suspected, only if an arrest is made. Therefore, no one knows anything officially about the offenders who in 1968 committed the 80 percent of those recorded crimes for which no arrests were made. This poses a knotty problem for the scientist, since all we know officially about juvenile delinquency, or the criminality of males and females, blacks and whites, the poor and the rich, comes from what we learn about the conduct and the characteristics of persons arrested, prosecuted, or convicted. It is highly probable that those who are arrested do not completely resemble those who were never caught.

In recent years, sociologists have, indeed, made many surveys in order to discover to what extent official statistics of delinquency and delinquents match the reality. Using questionnaires or interviews, they have uncovered some interesting facts. They have learned that practically no one grows up completely innocent of lawbreaking and that the risk of being caught and labeled a delinquent is not the same for all social classes or neighborhoods. Therefore, the officially known delinquent is not representative of all delinquents. This is documented in the articles by Maynard L. Erickson and LaMar T. Empey and by Irving Piliavin and Scott Briar. They found that the police were not even-handed in the enforcement of the law, that boys who "looked tough," or were "sassy," or came from black neighborhoods were more likely to be arrested than boys who were neatly dressed, polite, and cooperative. Moreover, as Erickson and Empey learned from a sample including boys who had been to court and boys who had not, all admitted having committed various offenses. But the vast majority of the boys had escaped notice or, at least, a court record. The boys who had juvenile court records were such a small and select group that the authors concluded that such court records offered no sound basis for an index of delinquency.

Sociologists have been, of course, concerned with the social conditions and circumstances that produce delinquency and crime. Are these conditions to be found in the home life of a child, in the peer-group associations of a neighborhood, or elsewhere? Research has usually revealed, for instance, that children from homes where parents are deviant or delinquent are more likely to get into trouble with the law than children from comparable homes where parents are law-abiding.

In a well-ordered, simpler society than ours, violations of the law would presumably be relatively few because the norms of the criminal law would be generally accepted as proper guidelines for conduct. In our complex urban-industrial society, however, many of the traditional middle-class norms that are reflected in the law are held in low esteem by various social groups, who may, indeed, cherish some norms which are even in direct conflict or opposition to the law. This condition is referred to by Cavan and is illustrated by Walter B. Miller, who spent several years in close contact with a score of youthful gangs in an eastern city. He found that people living in the slums, where these youths had been nurtured, had a traditional culture of their own. The gang members were found to share this culture's special concerns and attitudes; and the standards or norms upheld by the gang reflected them. Thus the boys, in being loyal to the norms of the slum culture, were in conflict with the law.

According to Richard A. Cloward and Lloyd E. Ohlin, slums not only breed delinquents at a high rate, but, because they differ in their social organization they also differ in the kind of delinquents they produce. These sociologists point out that some slum areas harbor so many professional criminals and an established network of shady businessmen ("fences," bookies, numbers banks) cooperating with them that juveniles or youths in gangs find it easy to graduate into professional or organized crime. In other slums, where the population is transient, social controls are weak, and where opportunities for joining the underworld or getting conventional jobs are few, the boys tend to form fighting gangs. A boy in either type of slum, if he cannot achieve status in a gang, may, depending on his personality, drift out of delinquency or take to drugs or alcohol.

Slums are the favorite but not exclusive breeding grounds of delinquent gangs. Larry Karacki and Jackson Toby describe a fighting and thieving gang of white upper-working-class and lower-middle-class boys from an average neighborhood. The story is instructive in showing that ganging is chiefly an adolescent venture. If some boys persist in their old delinquent ways, say the authors, it is due to their failure to develop early in life a commitment to adult roles and values. Gang membership offers them a substitute, and allegiance to the norms of the gang gives them a means of achieving status and recognition among peers who adopt the mode of life and standards of a "youth culture," which Joseph W. Scott and Edmund W. Vaz describe as something arising out of basic changes in American society in the last seventy-five years. They find much delinquent behavior outside of the slums.

The kind of crime committed by an individual depends, of course, in a measure on the social class to which the offender belongs. Poor people have little opportunity to embezzle trust funds, for instance, and those in comfortable circumstances are unlikely to burglarize houses or rob gas stations. Furthermore, urban slums have a tradition of delinquency which, together with the poverty of the slum dwellers, has generally been considered the direct or indirect cause of most delinquency and crime in our cities.

Many of the readings in this book would appear to lend some support to this belief, but they also demonstrate that the relationship of low social status to delinquency is a complicated question and not one that yields a simple answer. Albert J. Reiss, Jr., and Albert L. Rhodes found that the extent of the delinquency among low-class and middle-class boys, alike, depends in some degree on whether they attend schools in "poor" or "good" neighborhoods. The studies reported by Erwin Schepses and by Robert A. Dentler and Lawrence J. Monroe of young people who steal show that the car thieves are from middle-class homes as a rule and that the thefts admitted by junior high school students show no correlation with their social status.

The greatest challenge to the claim that poverty is the main cause of crime was made by Edwin H. Sutherland in his pioneering study of white-collar crime, which disclosed that the social damage of the criminality of the business community, as represented by large corporations, may be even greater than that of the poor classes of society. It would seem that each social group, whether a slum community or a business community, generates some congenial norms of conduct that flout the law.

Two of the readings, those by Earl Johnson, Jr., and John A. Gardiner, deal with a strange facet of American criminality, namely, organized crime. Some criminality in every country is professional in the sense that it requires special skills (counterfeiting, for instance) and means of converting the proceeds of a crime into profits (a "fence," for instance); but organized crime is different. As far as its structure is concerned, it is a business similar to other business enterprises and different only in that it is illegal or operates by illegal means. It is said to be one of the nation's greatest and wealthiest industries. An illustration of the kind of moral climate in which organized crime can successfully operate is found in Gardiner's story of the town he calls Wincanton.

Another characteristic of our national culture is described in John P. Spiegel's study of violence. It is an especially relevant article, considering the events of the present time. One aspect of violent protests in the streets is that during them, ordinarily law-abiding citizens find themselves in the role of lawbreakers. Anti-war demonstrations and student outbreaks bring a new class of offenders to the attention of the police. One consequence is a new standard of police behavior and new kinds of training for police officers.

The selection based on Richard A. Blum's review of drugs and drug users and the selection on alcoholics and their ways resemble the one on violence in that they all refer to deviant conduct which is not in itself criminal, but easily passes over into law-breaking. Thus research on alcoholics and drug addicts has a place in a book of readings on delinquency and crime, if it is understood that the behavior is a matter of degree and kind.

There is a growing awareness that our system of imprisonment fails, in the main, to rehabilitate prisoners and prepare them for a law-abiding life upon discharge. The selection based on Finestone's research shows how important it is that the social group to which the prisoner returns give him the moral support which he will need if he is to start out on a normal life. It also shows how necessary it is for those who operate prisons to take this into consideration when they devise correctional programs for prisoners from, for instance, the various ethnic groups.

The articles presented in this book are only a very small sample of sociological studies of crime and delinquency. The data assembled in them have been gathered by various methods, which show the way sociologists work. Some data have been gained by interviewing people, others by securing answers to questionnaires, still others by the technique of participant or direct observation. Personal observation was the method of Samuel E. Wallace and Earl Rubington in studying alcoholics. A common method of research—found several times in this book—is to take a sample of delinquents (the experimental group) and match them with a similar sample of nondelinquents (the control group). Knowing what nondelinquents or "normal" boys and girls are like serves as a base line for comparing the delinquents with them. The control group may be of youths picked from, for example, the same neighborhood or school, or of the same race, nationality, or age—depending on the investigator's intentions. Some authors have analyzed documents or records or already published works and have drawn their inferences from them. Ferdinand did this in studying crime in Boston. Blum studied public medical records on addicts. Scott and Vaz constructed their theory of middle-class delinquency on the research of a dozen sociologists who preceded them. Theory-building such as this is one more method by which science expands knowledge.

There are few specific suggestions about how crime and delinquency can be reduced, although the selections here may suggest preventive actions to the reader. Miller came to the conclusion that the delinquency of the slums is here to stay until the entire social fabric of the slum is changed, and this is hardly conceivable without fundamental social and economic transformations of American society. Thus the problem of delinquency and crime appears to him to involve matters like civil rights, rather than simply higher welfare allowances. Only a few sociologists say they know what should be done, but all sociologists agree that there must be bold measures, based on facts revealed by sound research. The research is their particular contribution to a very grave social problem.

What Is
Delinquent Behavior?*

What is juvenile delinquency?

Is it what the laws say, or is it behavior that a community decides it cannot tolerate?

Is there other behavior besides delinquency which the community considers intolerable?

Is the "overly good" child (one who cannot fit into normal society and who may be rejected because he demands perfection from others) a delinquent? Can we place all behavior on a line running from crime to perfection, with most people belonging halfway between?

What is juvenile delinquency?

Were Marian Dean and Sally Schwartz delinquent when—just once in their lives—they walked out of the five-and-ten with a pocketful of lipsticks they hadn't paid for?

Were Harry Farley and the boys with him delinquent last Halloween when they tore the mail boxes from a dozen front doors and painted stripes on the doors of three garages?

And what about Tommy Jones when the police caught him breaking into the parking meters on Second Street? And Bill Smathers, who comes to school only three days out of five? And Grace Daugherty, who peddles dope to her sophomore classmates?

In defining juvenile delinquency, laws are of limited usefulness. Usually laws are specific only about serious adult offenses such as murder, assault, and robbery. Children are considered delinquent if they are found guilty in court of breaking these laws. But such serious offenses account for only a small proportion of

* Adapted from "The Concepts of Tolerance and Contraculture as Applied to Delinquency" by Ruth Shonle Cavan, *Sociological Quarterly*, Vol. 2 (1961), pp. 243–258. Reprinted by permission.

juvenile delinquencies. Most acts that get youngsters into trouble with the law come under a much less definite part of the law. For example, the Illinois law (as of 1965) defined a delinquent as a child who has violated or attempted to violate a federal or state law or a municipal ordinance or a lawful court order; also in need of supervision is any minor who is beyond the control of his parents, guardian, or other custodian, or who is habitually truant from school. Laws in other states are equally vague. New Mexico bases its definition on the word *habitual:* a delinquent is one who is *habitually* uncontrolled, *habitually* disobedient, *habitually* wayward; or who is *habitually* a truant; or who *habitually* deports himself in a way that endangers the morals, health, or welfare of himself or others. In these laws, however, there is no definition of *habitual,* or of *incorrigible,* or of *indecent* conduct.

In an effort to clarify matters, the federal Children's Bureau has defined juvenile delinquency cases as those which are referred to court for violation of certain laws or for conduct so seriously antisocial as to interfere with the rights of others or to menace the welfare of the community or of the delinquent himself. But while this helps a little, it does not say what guidelines adults are to use in deciding when a child's behavior justifies a court hearing or if a court hearing is the only measure of delinquency. Are there gradations of delinquency? And if so, at what point does misbehavior become delinquency?

The problem of reaching a basic definition of juvenile delinquency has engaged the attention of many people. One of the most interesting answers has been offered by an Illinois sociologist, Dr. Ruth Shonle Cavan. Her conclusion is that juvenile behavior, and adult behavior as well, is not a matter of simple good and bad as many people say it is. There are, rather, gradations in behavior and also in delinquency.

The bell-shaped diagram is Dr. Cavan's picture of the way people in any society behave. According to her theory, human behavior ranges from disapproved, *non*conforming behavior (A) through a lesser degree of disapproved *under*conforming behavior (B and C), until D is reached. D stands for normal behavior. But behavior can take the opposite direction, through increasing degrees of *over*conforming good conduct (E and F) to near perfection at G. The numbers of people falling into each of these areas rises from A to D and then declines to G. The normal (D) is the modal behavior of most people. Very few behave in ways that would classify them in the extremes (A or G).

Even though we know that behavior falls along a continuous line (what scientists call a continuum), nevertheless we tend to think in terms of two poles. We have the sinner and the saint, the devil and the angel, the alcoholic and the teetotaler, the criminal and the upright citizen, the juvenile delinquent and the model child. We tend to force behavior into a pair of pure extremes, the

FIGURE 1

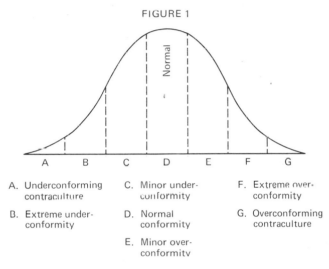

A	B	C	D	E	F	G

A. Underconforming contraculture

B. Extreme under-conformity

C. Minor under-conformity

D. Normal conformity

E. Minor over-conformity

F. Extreme over-conformity

G. Overconforming contraculture

totally evil and the completely perfect. We forget the many gradations of behavior in between. In delinquency, from A to G in Figure 1, we might have serious offenses such as nighttime burglary; daytime shoplifting; occasional pilfering; tolerated borrowing and failure to return (D or tolerated behavior); meticulous avoidance of taking things; remonstrance with others who steal; or reporting of other children to teachers or police for even minor pilfering (G).

The small gradations make it easy for a person to slip from tolerated misdeeds to slightly more serious misconduct until serious offenses become habitual. Reversing the process, however, is difficult.

We do not really expect or require anyone to be completely good or right. Seeing that man is not perfect—that he cannot always obey all the rules—society makes concessions to his imperfections. Behavior in D is looked on as acceptable and normal within flexible working limits: as long as it does not overstep the bounds too far and as long as it does not threaten the social organization itself. Thus, for example, a recent study made in an electronics plant revealed that repairmen and others often helped themselves to small parts and took them home. They explained that no one thought of this as thievery: "It's *our* company," explained one worker. "The plant doesn't need all these supplies," said another. "It can't be wrong," explained a third, "because the foreman helped me find what I wanted. The foremen expect it and do it, too." There is, in short, in D an area of toleration. Thus D, the normal, is not complete and rigid conformity but is, rather, reasonably well-restrained behavior. *Under*conformity (A, B, and C) is an exaggeration of the *tolerance* allowed by D, while E, F, and G represent degrees of excessive strictness in observing the norms of D.

The kind of boy and girl in D may occasionally neglect to return small things they borrow, play truant once or twice, mark up the walls of a rival high school, do a little damage to private property under the stress of excitement, lie to their own advantage, neglect their chores at home, and "sass" their parents. But they never go too far. Consequently, they receive the general approval of society. Their failings are looked upon as childish weaknesses which they can be expected to outgrow in time.

Young people in C and E, however, deviate just enough from the accepted standards of behavior (D) to make their elders worry about them. Although they do not pose a serious threat to society, there is some anxiety lest they may. The general attitude toward them, therefore, is toleration without approval. Efforts to correct or prevent their failings and misdeeds are usually handled by parents or school authorities. More attention is given to the underconformers than to the overconformers. The latter, however, are frequently warned to "get in the swing of things" and not to interfere with other people's fun.

The behavior of boys and girls in B and F is definitely disapproved. The chronic truant in B upsets the smooth operation of his school. At the extreme, the girl in F who is always perfectly prepared and instantly puts up her hand to answer every question or who is always available after school to do the schoolroom chores is also a hindrance because she discourages others from doing their share. Sometimes this sort of girl is unpopular—which puzzles her because she is conscientiously and unfailingly doing "the right thing."

Although the underconformers in B are scolded and punished for violating accepted standards of behavior, they are welcomed as friends and playmates by those in D. Police warn or arrest them but do not necessarily refer them to juvenile court. The school may suspend them but does not expel them. In short, wherever they go, they are made to feel that they are in some danger of being rejected, but they never are.

The overconforming youths in F are handled somewhat differently. The usual attitude toward them is one of impatience, sometimes one of scorn. They, too, are made to feel that they are on the outer margins of society. They are excluded from many cliques and from games and sports because they are "spoil sports," "tattletales," and "goody-goods." Adults, if they take any action, try to stimulate their interest in more normal youthful activities and attitudes to life and to others. Sometimes the overconformers are referred to psychiatric clinics for diagnosis and treatment.

B and F youths themselves feel they are not solidly rooted in the social structure. They waver between adjusting to the normal behavior patterns of D and abandoning them altogether. They feel alternately wanted and rejected by those in D. If they sense that they are being rejected, the underconformers grow hostile, and they show their hostility by stealing, vandalism, and various kinds of attack. The overconformers become shrilly critical. But the B's and the F's, if they consider the gestures made toward them by representatives of D are friendly, may be won over to the conforming groups. In fact, Dr. Cavan declares that if youth who are in B are to be rescued from falling into delinquency, the attempts at reclamation should be started while they are still in B, before they drop into A. Youth in area F do not tend to become delinquent, but because they are overly critical and intolerant of others they also need to be drawn back into D. Too often nonconformers are simply punished. This may alienate them further from D and drive them to A and G, which is the very opposite of restoring them to the approval of society.

Young people in groups A and G differ from all others in that their behavior does not simply deviate from accepted standards but is actually opposed to them. Those who belong in A are condemned by society not only for their behavior but also as persons. They are known as punks, hoodlums, hard-core delinquents. They are likely to be expelled from school and often are committed to correctional school or even prison. Very occasionally such a delinquent receives the death penalty.

For their part, the youths reject society. They no longer measure their behavior against normally accepted standards; instead, their standards are the opposite of D. They are the values of the gang with whom they associate or of criminals whom they admire. They take pride in stealing, chronic truancy, fighting. And efforts to change them are usually unavailing.

Similarly, those in G are at odds with society. Rejected by even their own peers, as well as by their seniors because of their overconformity and because of their holier-than-thou attitudes, they create their own little society. They do not threaten the larger society in the same way as the delinquents, but they may develop a different philosophy of life which they regard as better or more idealistic than the normal, or D, way of life which most people accept. Sometimes they simply withdraw from the larger society into informal cliques or clubs. But others, especially older teen-agers, may actively try to reform or drastically change the larger society by protests, such as burning draft cards, rioting, destroying property, or violent fighting. Since these acts are violations of laws, these overconformers are often arrested. Adults in G may go to extremes to try to make society better according to their own ideas. Carrie Nation, who rampaged through cities a century ago smashing saloon windows, was a zealot, an overconformer who tolerated no exception to what she thought was right. In so doing she found herself in violent opposition to the normal, or D, portion of society.

Those classified under both G and A have set up their own standards or culture. Dr. Cavan speaks of these two deviant systems of values as "contracultures." Persons of the A or G type measure their behavior by their contracultures, and no longer by

Stages of Continuity in Behavior

	A	B	C	D	E	F	G
	DELINQUENT CONTRACULTURE	EXTREME UNDER-CONFORMITY	MINOR UNDER-CONFORMITY	NORMAL CONFORMITY	MINOR OVER-CONFORMITY	EXTREME OVER-CONFORMITY	OVERCONFORMING CONTRA-CULTURE
Public attitude	Condemnation; "hard core"	Disapproval	Toleration without approval	Tolerance with approval	Toleration without approval	Disapproval	Condemnation
Public reaction	Rejection; school expulsion; correctional school	Police warnings; school suspension; referral to social agency	Disciplinary action by school or parent	Indifference; acceptance; mild reproofs	Ignoring	Ostracizing	Rejection
Child's attitude toward public	Rejection of values of D	Wavering between acceptance and rejection of D values	Acceptance of values of D; feelings of guilt	Acceptance of D; no guilt feelings	No deviation in personal conduct	Criticism of D behavior in others	Rejection of D values
Child's self-concept	As delinquent; outlaw	Confused, marginal to C and A	As misbehaving nondelinquent	Conforming nondelinquent	As a true conformer	Better than others	His way is the only right way
Examples	Armed robbery; burglary	Larceny of valuables	"Borrowing" and keeping; pilfering	Minor pilfering; unauthorized borrowing	Borrowing only with permission	No borrowing; criticism of others	Report even minor pilfering to teacher or police
	Drug addiction	Occasional use of drugs	Smoking of marijuana	Smoking tobacco	No smoking	No stimulating drinks, even tea or coffee	Opposition to use by others

D. In fact, they are indifferent or even vengeful toward D. These characteristics from A to G along the continuum of behavior appear in the table, which brings out the differences between the types.

Dr. Cavan's analysis of the way people behave helps to clarify several problems connected with juvenile delinquency:

1. Each social class has its own rules about what constitutes acceptable and unacceptable behavior, what falls within the area of tolerance and what is disapproved of, mildly or severely. Figure 2 illustrates in a very rough way how members of the lower class and middle class view the seven areas of behavior from A to G. On the greater part, that is, on modal behavior, the classes agree, by and large. But at the extremes the lower class tolerates some A behavior that is unacceptable to the middle class. And the middle class will put up with behavior of the G type which the lower class would condemn.

FIGURE 2

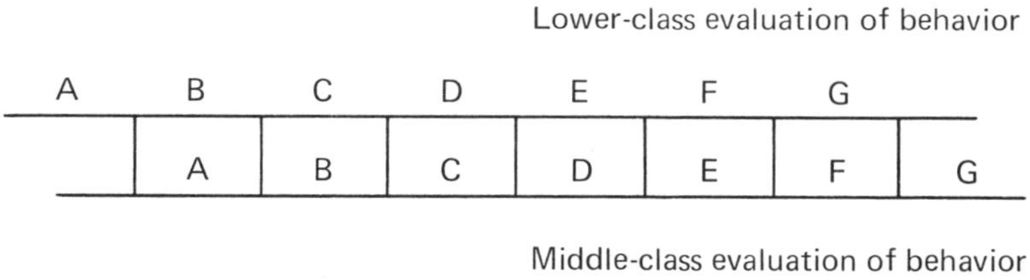

Lower-class evaluation of behavior

A	B	C	D	E	F	G	
	A	B	C	D	E	F	G

Middle-class evaluation of behavior

For example, take the case of the father whose son was in a correctional school for taking a car to go joy riding. The father said, "Of course, he took a few cars, but he did not strip them; he just wanted to use them. He is not a bad boy." But in the eyes of the judge, the boy had stolen the cars. The middle-class judge —and the law—condemn certain acts as of the A type, but the boy and his father looked upon his deed as B or even C. Thus a wide range of everyday lower-class behavior is condemned by the middle class.

2. Precisely because each class views behavior of the extreme types (A and B, F and G) in its own way, certain problems arise in dealing with delinquency. School, police, and court authorities generally belong to the middle class and often do not

understand the behavior of the lower class; nor, as just noted, do they share its values. Consequently, when a delinquent youth comes up for parole or is put on probation, his movements are often so restricted by the court that he finds it almost impossible to conform to them. Sooner or later he is in trouble again. The same boy might, says Dr. Cavan, have a better chance if what is required during parole is behavior more in line with his class standards.

3. It is often said that all boys are delinquent but only poor boys wind up in court. And it is true that much delinquent behavior on the part of middle- and upper-class boys and girls *is* largely overlooked: they are not arrested and they are not taken to the juvenile court. But recent studies by two sociologists of Washington State University, F. Ivan Nye and James F. Short, Jr., make it clear that youths who are sent to correctional schools (the great majority of them are poor) far outstrip ordinary high school students in the seriousness and frequency of their offenses. For example, whereas *half* the high school boys and girls had skipped school at least once, the study showed that *all* the boys and girls in the correctional school had done so. Similarly, whereas 5 percent of the high school students had at some time stolen something worth $50 or more, the figure for the group in the correctional school was 90 percent. In short, whereas the high school students had confined the greater part of their delinquencies to acts within the area of tolerance, D, or at most C, the young people in the correctional school were guilty of types A and B behavior.

In summary: Dr. Cavan represented behavior as ranging along a continuum running from an *under*conforming *contra*culture through various degrees of disapproved behavior to normal conformity and then through stages of overconforming behavior to an *over*conforming *contra*culture. The reaction of the normally conforming segment of the population to deviations A to C and E to G is mild or severe according to how much the social norms are threatened by either underconformity or overconformity. Minor deviants usually are drawn back into conformity. Serious deviants often are treated so severely that they are alienated and withdraw into a contraculture.

Who Is a Delinquent
and Who Is Not?*

How does a policeman exercise discretion in arresting a juvenile?

What features of a juvenile's behavior will make it likely that a policeman will merely scold him? What will make it likely that the policeman will arrest him?

What is the effect of these two different reactions of the policeman upon the statistics of delinquency?

Denny Edwards had just turned the key of the Buick when he was blinded by the glare of a flashlight. At the same time, the rear view mirror above him showed the whirling blue light of a police car. The officer on the sidewalk opened the door of the Buick and looked closely at the boy in the driver's seat.

"Is this your car?" the policeman asked as he motioned for Denny to get out.

"Nope." Denny slouched against the fender of the car and snapped his fingers to an imaginary tune.

"Then what were you doing in it? How old are you?" As he questioned Denny, the officer opened a black notebook and began recording information from the driver's license the boy had given him. The policeman noted, too, the leather jacket emblazoned with the crest of the Dragons, a local teen-age gang. "And stop snapping your fingers when I'm talking to you!" he said severely.

Denny shrugged and looked up resignedly. "I was just sitting here waiting for someone."

"Does he own the car?" the officer inquired somewhat impatiently.

* Adapted from "Police Encounters with Juveniles" by Irving Piliavin and Scott Briar, *American Journal of Sociology* (The University of Chicago Press), Vol. 70, No. 2 (September 1964), pp. 206–214. Reprinted by permission.

"No, I don't know whose it is, but the dumb jerk left his keys." Denny's words were accompanied by more finger snapping, and his black face was almost expressionless.

The officer was silent as he made a few more notes. Then he pointed to the waiting squad car.

"OK, Denny, get in the car."

The boy's nonchalance quickly vanished. "What for ? *I* didn't do nothing!" he protested. The fingers that had been snapping were now clenched in a fist; the boredom left his face and was replaced by anger.

"If we hadn't come along this car would be miles from here," the policeman replied. "Now move!"

About six blocks away, another boy reached for the ignition of a station wagon. He was backing slowly out of the parking space when he became aware of a vehicle moving towards him. Carl Morris recognized the shape of a police car, and he hastily drove the car forward into its original position. As he opened the car door, Carl heard the officer's voice, ordering him to come out.

Carl trembled visibly as he looked up and saw the policeman's hand held out for the boy's driver's license. "I don't have one," Carl stuttered. "I wasn't going anywhere. I just wanted to see how the car felt."

The officer looked at the blond youngster standing in front of him. "How old are you, son?" the policeman asked in a gruff but not unkind voice.

"Thirteen, sir," Carl replied, nearly crying. "And my father will kill me if I get in trouble!"

The boy was dressed in clean chino pants and a plaid wool shirt. The fear in his face was plain to see.

"Then stay away from other people's cars," the policeman barked, closing his notebook without having written anything. "Don't you ever let me see you here again. Do you understand?"

"Yes, sir," Carl stammered. "Are you going to arrest me?"

"Not this time, but you be careful! Now go straight home, right now!"

The officer's final words followed Carl as he raced away.

Some very important questions are raised by these two meetings between police and juveniles. Why is Denny Edwards sitting sullenly in police headquarters while Carl Morris is hurrying home? The two boys committed much the same offense at the same time in the same city and yet they were treated very differently by law enforcement officers. Why? And with what consequences? Are either or both of them "juvenile delinquents"?

Realizing the seriousness of these questions, two California sociologists, Irving Piliavin and Scott Briar, went to a metropolitan police department to observe encounters with juveniles. The setting of the investigation was an industrial city of about 450,000 inhabitants, served by a police force which was widely known for its honesty and its superior personnel.

In the police department, the officers of the Juvenile Bureau were the elite. Because a Juvenile Officer was expected to be responsible for the prevention of delinquency as well as for law enforcement and to be familiar with conditions leading to crime and delinquency, assignment to the Juvenile Bureau was considered an indication of a man's high quality as an officer of the law.

Piliavin and Briar concentrated their attention on this select group of policemen for nine months in the early 1960s, observing the officers during their regular tours of duty. They accompanied officers on duty, observed them dealing with juveniles at headquarters, and made notes on all they saw. They found that the Juvenile Officers, who operated essentially as patrolmen, cruising along assigned beats, confronted a juvenile offender in one of the following three ways, listed in order of increasing frequency: they "spotted" an officially "wanted" youth; they were at or near the scene of an offense reported to police headquarters; or, on their own, they observed a youth either committing an offense or acting "suspiciously."

The meetings between both Denny and Carl and the police were clearly examples of boys being spotted while engaged in a questionable activity. Why, then, did the officers act so differently?

Part of the answer, the two sociologists discovered, lay in the fact that a policeman dealing with a youthful offender was allowed to decide between a wide choice of ways to deal with any given situation. The nature of the offense itself was only one circumstance influencing the officer's decision, and other criteria were extremely important when a policeman was faced with the problem of handling a wayward juvenile.

The officers who found Denny and Carl in cars which did not belong to them could have dealt with the boys in any one of the following ways:

1. They could have released them outright.

2. They could have released them and submitted a "field interrogation report" briefly describing the circumstances that brought the boys to their attention.

3. They could have let them off with an "official reprimand" and released them to their parents or guardian.

4. They could have cited them to the juvenile court.

5. They could have arrested them and confined them in Juvenile Hall.

In the case of the first two alternatives, the matter ended there. But alternatives three, four, and five differ from one and two in two basic respects. First, with rare exceptions, when an officer chose to reprimand, cite, or arrest a boy, he took the youth to the police station. Second, the reprimanded, cited, or arrested boy acquired an official police "record"; that is, his name was entered on the files of the Juvenile Bureau as a juvenile offender.

Piliavin and Briar discovered that the full range of alternatives was indeed used by officers. One reason for the flexibility of the police was their reluctance to expose certain youths to the stigma of official police action. Few members of the Juvenile Unit believed that correctional agencies could really help delinquents, and all the officers were convinced that the processes of justice were essentially focused on punishment rather than on rehabilitation. Further, members of the Juvenile Bureau were sure that such possible consequences of police action as rejection by parents, school, and peers, intimate contact with "hard-core" delinquents, and the community's definition of delinquency could reinforce what might only have been budding delinquent behavior. Thus, unless officers were sure that a youth was really committed to deviant behavior, they were inclined to treat him leniently.

The policy of the Juvenile Officers was to deal with a youthful offender on the basis of what seemed best for him. Giving the officers some freedom of action was unofficially justified by the fact that strict enforcement of laws in every case would not only increase the load of the juvenile courts, but overcrowd detention facilities and dramatically increase juvenile crime rates—situations to be avoided since they would expose the police department to public criticism.

Permitting discretion and flexibility in coping with juveniles posed several problems to the police. First, an officer had to be able to justify his course of action in view of the nature of the offense and the character of the offender. Consequently, a policeman often found himself making what was, in effect, a *judicial* decision, for by reprimanding and releasing a young offender, the officer could actually punish him without submitting his case to the court. Finally, since no explicit rules existed for resolving each situation, policemen often felt uncertain and uncomfortable about what steps they should take. In spite of these difficulties, Juvenile Officers continued to decide what course to take on the basis of the "character" of apprehended youths.

How were the policemen able to form opinions about the personalities and life situations of the young people with whom they had contact? Piliavin and Briar found that, in the matter of serious crime, at least, patrolmen had relatively little trouble determining the "character" of the offender. Such violations as robbery, homicide, aggravated assault, grand theft, auto theft, and arson were generally thought to be committed by confirmed delinquents. In the case of minor offenders, however, who comprised over 90 percent of the youths against whom police took action, the act itself played a comparatively small part in the officer's decision. Generally, he based his action on the impression the boy made on him—on whether he seemed to be a hardened delinquent or merely a "good" boy temporarily gone astray.

Unfortunately, police officers had little access to information about a youth at the moment when a choice had to be made about taking him to the police station. Furthermore, files at headquarters provided data only about each offender's prior record. Thus, both in the field and at the station, the police had to base their decisions on clues which emerged at the time in the interaction between themselves and the young person—clues from which they might infer the youth's character. The clues included the boy's membership in clubs or gangs, his age, race, grooming, dress, and demeanor or attitude. Older juveniles, members of known delinquent gangs, blacks, youths who have very long hair, black leather jackets, and soiled denims or jeans, and boys who did not show the proper signs of respect toward authority were the most likely to receive harsh treatment.

Other than the record of his earlier behavior, the most important clue was a youth's attitude. In fact, the juvenile officers themselves said that attitude and bearing were a major influence in between 50 and 60 percent of the juvenile cases with which they dealt. There was a marked association between a "cooperative" attitude in the juvenile and leniency on the part of the police. Among 66 youths whose encounters with the police Piliavin and Briar observed, only 2 who were "cooperative" were arrested, in contrast to 14 who were "uncooperative" (See table).

Police Treatment, According to Youth's Demeanor

SEVERITY OF POLICE DISPOSITION	YOUTH'S DEMEANOR		
	COOPERATIVE	UNCOOPERATIVE	TOTAL
Arrest (most severe)	2	14	16
Citation or Official Reprimand	4	5	9
Informal Reprimand	15	1	16
Admonition and Release (least severe)	24	1	25
Total	45	21	66

The notes kept by the two sociologists show the importance which the police attached to demeanor:

In interrogating "A" (an 18-year-old upper-lower-class white male), certain points positively affected the sergeant's judgment. First, the youth was polite and cooperative; he consistently addressed the officer as "sir," and he answered all questions quietly and signed a statement implicating himself in numerous offenses.

Furthermore, the youth was not in fact a member of a gang of which the police disapproved. The sergeant's attitude became increasingly sympathetic and he announced that he intended to "get 'A' off the hook."

Two officers brought into the police station a 17-year-old white boy, along with two older companions. The boy responded to police officers' questions slowly and with obvious indifference. It was apparent that his lack of deference and his failure to show concern were irritating them. Finally, one of the police, turning to the boy, exclaimed, "What am I going to do with you?" The boy simply returned the officer's gaze. The latter then said, "Well, I guess we'll just have to put you away for a while." An arrest report was then made out and the boy was taken to Juvenile Hall.

Besides attitude, Piliavin and Briar noted two other significant clues: race and the "delinquent stereotype." Compared to other youths, blacks and boys who "looked tough" were most frequently stopped and questioned by patrolmen—often in the absence of any evidence of wrongdoing—and usually were dealt with more severely for the same offenses. The clearest evidence of this was provided by the over-representation of blacks among "innocent" juveniles accosted by the police. Of the 76 juveniles on whom systematic data were collected, 10 were released without suspicion. Seven, or two-thirds of these 10 "innocent" juveniles were black, in contrast to the allegedly "guilty" youths, less than one-third of whom were black.

Was such discrimination simply the result of long-held personal prejudices on the part of individual policemen? Eighteen of twenty-seven officers interviewed openly admitted a dislike for black people. However, they explained that their feelings resulted from experiences they had had as policemen with black youths. Constant exposure to uncooperative black juveniles had, according to the officers, caused their antipathy towards the whole race. As one policeman stated it:

> Many of these kids have no regard for the law or for the police. They seem to have absolutely no respect for you as an adult. I admit I am prejudiced now, but frankly, I don't think I was when I began police work.

Such candidly expressed bias was only part of the reason why officers dealt with certain youths more often and more severely than they did with others. They justified concentrating on particular neighborhoods, gangs, and individuals by claiming that they were directing their attention especially towards the youths whom they believed were most likely to commit delinquent acts. A highly placed official in the department told the sociologists:

> If you know that the bulk of your delinquent problem comes from kids who, say, are from 12 to 14 years of age, when you're out on patrol you are much more likely to be sensitive to the activities of juveniles in this age bracket than of older or younger groups. This would be good law enforcement practice. The logic in our case is the same except that our delinquency problem is largely found in the black community and it is these youths towards whom we are sensitized.

The two sociologists summed up their observations as follows:

First, the Juvenile Officers are allowed and even urged to be very flexible in deciding what to do with youthful offenders. In choosing their course of action, they are strongly guided by the attitude of the youths who are involved. As a result, they treat certain boys (blacks, "tough guys," and the like) more severely than other juveniles, even though the offense is the same. Since the more serious penalties result in a "record," the police statistics appear to justify the officers' suspicion of these particular types of offenders. In the end, then, "justice" is not the same for all.

The discriminatory practice of the police, even if based on accurate statistical evidence, becomes part of a vicious circle. If officers watch and question the same boy several times, he is likely to grow hostile, especially if he is actually innocent of wrongdoing. Furthermore, after several meetings with the police, a youth is liable to regard the encounters as "routine," and consequently he may act as if somewhat bored, a response which police associate with hard-core delinquency. And, since a boy who is often observed or "picked up" generally displays a "bad attitude," it is very likely that he will be dealt with severely, should he commit an offense. Then, as a recorded delinquent, he becomes part of the statistical evidence cited by police to justify their original surveillance.

To a large extent, the Juvenile Officers' practice of observing and punishing some youthful offenders more than others is an extension of the juvenile court's philosophy that a young person should be handled according to *what is best for him*, rather than according to *what he did*. The theory is well meant, but the objection to it is that decisions made by police on the basis of a youth's character are not controlled by impersonal restrictions which would protect the juvenile from possible prejudice on the part of the police.

Finally, the observations made by Piliavin and Briar underscored an important fact: A youth becomes a "juvenile delinquent" because someone in authority has defined him as one, and the definition is often more on the basis of his color or attitude or demeanor than on the offense he has committed. So Carl Morris will go home, a juvenile who has been involved in a delinquent act and let off with a warning. Denny Edwards will spend the night in Juvenile Hall, and the records will show that he is a "juvenile delinquent."

How Much Delinquency Is There?*

How much more delinquency would there be if we could know all the offenses that are never detected?

What offenses are ones which most often are not found out?

Do the boys who commit the undiscovered offenses commit as many offenses as the boys whose offenses are discovered?

As guidance counselor at Lakewood High School, Mr. Chambers was investigating the vandalism and petty theft which had been disrupting the school. By the time he had interviewed several boys about the incidents, Mr. Chambers realized that his ideas about the extent of delinquency in the community had been entirely wrong. Like many others, the guidance counselor had assumed that the police reports were a fairly complete and accurate record of the unlawful behavior of the community's youth. However, Mr. Chambers discovered that most of the students involved in the trouble at the school had never appeared in court.

Several boys had candidly described numerous escapades of shoplifting, gambling, and drinking which had gone undetected by those in authority. One boy, for example, enumerated over 40 incidents of lawless behavior, none of which had ever appeared in an official record. He lived in a nice neighborhood, wore good clothes, and was polite, the boy explained, and the police paid little attention to what he and his friends did during their leisure time. Most of the juvenile officers concentrated on the "tough kids" and largely ignored many other high school students.

* Adapted from "Court Records, Undetected Delinquency, and Decision-Making" by Maynard L. Erickson and LaMar T. Empey, *Journal of Criminal Law, Criminology, and Police Science*, Vol. 54 (December 1963), pp. 456–469; and from "Hidden Delinquency and Social Status" by LaMar T. Empey and Maynard L. Erickson, *Social Forces* (Chapel Hill, N.C.: University of North Carolina Press), Vol. 44, No. 4 (June 1966), pp. 546–554. Reprinted by permission.

When the last of the "suspects" had been interviewed, Mr. Chambers compared his list with the names of the boys who were considered by the police and school to be officially "delinquent." * Without exception, not one of the students who appeared to be guilty of the thefts and vandalism was listed in the police files. It was now clear to Mr. Chambers that the greater part of the delinquency in the community was undetected and that the official police reports took no account of it.

Concern and confusion over the gap between the official data on delinquency and the actual extent of it are shared by many community authorities and by sociologists, particularly those who specialize in criminology. How, experts wonder, can programs be designed to prevent delinquency if the problem is regarded in the light of incomplete and possibly misleading information? If many juvenile offenses are not part of court records, what are the real facts about the extent of juvenile delinquency?

In order to explore this question, two sociologists, Maynard L. Erickson and LaMar T. Empey at Brigham Young University in Utah, set up a research project on the nature and extent of undetected offenses in a selected population of adolescent boys. The knowledge they might glean from their small sample would give them some hints of the facts of delinquency in general. The sociologists point out, however, that the young people they studied were nearly all Mormons. Members of a conservative church in an authoritarian society, they could be expected to be more respectful of the law than big-city youths whose lives are freer from control by family and community.†

Erickson and Empey began their research by raising the following questions:

1. *What is revealed about the total volume of delinquency when undetected offenses are counted in? What offenses are most common among those that never come to official attention?*

2. *How much delinquency goes undetected and unacted upon in the courts?*

---

* See "Who Is a Delinquent and Who Is Not?" in this book.
† See "The Slum: Opportunities for Crime and Delinquency" in this book.

3. Do young delinquents who have never been caught commit as many delinquencies as the young offenders who are found out? And are their delinquent acts equally serious?

4. How useful are the customary classifications—delinquent or nondelinquent, institutionalized or noninstitutionalized—in distinguishing groups of offenders from one another?

5. How reliable are court records as an indication of the total volume and the types of offenses in which young people are commonly involved?

Selecting a sample totaling 180 boys between 15 and 17 years of age, the two sociologists divided them into four subsamples: (1) a subsample of 50 high school boys who had never been to court; (2) a subsample of 30 boys who had been to court once; (3) a subsample of 50 recidivists (the word meaning repeat offenders) who were on probation, 16 of whom would have been in jail had they not been in a special community program; and (4) a subsample of 50 offenders who were incarcerated (imprisoned) in correctional institutions. The boys in the first three subsamples were randomly chosen from one county in Utah; those in the fourth were picked from among the whole Utah population of youths in correctional institutions. All of these boys were questioned personally by the sociologists about how many and what kind of offenses they had committed.

What was the most effective method by which to collect data from the young respondents? As some of the boys were nearly illiterate and found it hard to understand the questions, Erickson and Empey decided that interviewing might be the soundest method of learning the facts of delinquency. By using three skilled interviewers who could anticipate problems and understand not only what the boys were trying to say but their wordless gestures as well, the sociologists sought to reduce hindrances to easy communication and to gain the youths' confidence.

But in spite of all the interviewers did to put them at their ease, the boys were reluctant to reveal delinquent activities which had not been detected by the authorities. Moreover, some boys found it hard to remember how many times they had committed a certain offense. But long and relaxed discussion helped the interviewers to arrive at reasonably accurate estimates.

TABLE 1
Amount of Delinquency by Offense—Percent Undetected and Percent Not Acted Upon

OFFENSE	RANK	ENTIRE ADOLESCENT SAMPLE			SUBSAMPLES (1) 50 NONDELINQUENTS		
		TOTAL OFFENSES	UNDE-TECTED	UNACTED UPON	TOTAL OFFENSES	UNDE-TECTED	UNACTED UPON
THEFT:	1						
Articles less than $2		15,175	97%	100%	966	92%	100%
Articles worth $2 to $50		7,396	97	99	60	83	100
Articles more than $50		294	71	93	1	100	100
Auto theft		822	89	95	4	100	100
Forgery		512	93	97	0	0	0
Total		24,199	96	99	1,031	91	100
OFFENSES INVOLVING ALCOHOL AND NARCOTICS:	2						
Buying beer or liquor		8,890	100	100	18	100	100
Drinking beer or liquor		12,808	99	100	219	100	100
Selling narcotics		1	100	100	0	0	0
Using narcotics		74	100	100	0	0	0
Total		21,773	99	100	237	100	100

TABLE 1 (continued)

OFFENSE	RANK	ENTIRE ADOLESCENT SAMPLE			SUBSAMPLES (1) 50 Nondelinquents		
		TOTAL OFFENSES	UNDE-TECTED	UNACTED UPON	TOTAL OFFENSES	UNDE-TECTED	UNACTED UPON
OFFENSES AGAINST PROPERTY:	3						
Breaking and entering		1,622	86	94	67	94	100
Destroying property		10,645	98	100	477	97	100
Setting fires (arson)		11	40	90	2	0	0
Total		12,278	97	99	546	97	100
TRAFFIC OFFENSES:	4						
Driving without license		11,796	99	100	1,845	100	100
OFFENSES AGAINST THE PERSON:	5						
Armed robbery		46	80	91	0	0 *	0
Fighting, assault		8,980	100	100	354	100 *	100
Total		9,026	100	100	354	100 *	100

TABLE 1 (continued)

		(2) 50 One-Time Offenders †			(3) 50 Delinquents in the Community			(4) 50 Delinquents Incarcerated		
OFFENSE	RANK	TOTAL OFFENSES	UNDE-TECTED	UNACTED UPON	TOTAL OFFENSES	UNDE-TECTED	UNACTED UPON	TOTAL OFFENSES	UNDE-TECTED	UNACTED UPON
THEFT:	1									
Articles less than $2		1,738	96%	100%	7,886	99%	100%	4,585	96%	100%
Articles worth $2 to $50		80	94	96	4,671	98	99	2,585	95	99
Articles more than $50		2	100	100	90	67	91	201	73	93
Auto theft		0	0	0	169	85	93	649	90	96
Forgery		0	0	0	60	70	90	452	96	98
Total		1,820	96	99	12,876	98	99	8,472	94	99
OFFENSES INVOLVING ALCOHOL AND NARCOTICS:	2									
Buying beer or liquor		57	94	100	1,453	100	100	7,362	100	100
Drinking beer or liquor		270	100	100	4,173	99	100	8,146	99	100
Selling narcotics		0	0	0	0	0	0	1	100	100
Using narcotics		0	0	0	3	100	100	71	100	100
Total		327	99	100	5,629	99	100	15,580	99	100

TABLE 1 (continued)

| | | (2) 50 One-Time Offenders† | | | (3) 50 Delinquents in the Community | | | (4) 50 Delinquents Incarcerated | | |
OFFENSE	RANK	TOTAL OFFENSES	UNDE-TECTED	UNACTED UPON	TOTAL OFFENSES	UNDE-TECTED	UNACTED UPON	TOTAL OFFENSES	UNDE-TECTED	UNACTED UPON
OFFENSES AGAINST PROPERTY:	3									
Breaking and entering		102	98	100	527	84	93	926	85	94
Destroying property		800	98	100	4,927	99	100	4,441	99	99
Setting fires (arson)		2	0	100	0	0	0	7	100	100
Total		904	96	100	5,454	97	99	5,374	96	98
TRAFFIC OFFENSES:	4									
Driving without license		512	99	99	2,386	98	99	7,053	99	100
OFFENSES AGAINST THE PERSON:	5									
Armed robbery		0	0	0	22	68	91	24	92	92
Fighting, assault		103	100 *	100	2,207	100 *	100	6,316	100 *	100
Total		103	100 *	100	2,229	97 *	100	6,340	99 *	100

SUBSAMPLES

* Because of their nature, these offenses almost never remain undetected by someone in authority. Thus, these figures refer to percent *not arrested*, rather than *undetected*.

† This class actually contained thirty cases. To make it possible to compare it with the other groups, which all contained 50, the sociologists inflated the 30 to 50 by multiplying all the totals for this group by two-fifths.

However, as the interviews went on, the sociologists became alert to a bias in the boys' statements which could make them less reliable. If, in the eyes of his peers, a boy could gain status by appearing to be delinquent, it would not be unusual for him to claim he had broken the law, although he had actually not done so. And, on the other hand, if delinquent behavior was not highly regarded by his particular group, a boy might attempt to pass over or make light of his own illegal activity.

In order to test the boys' answers, the sociologists looked in the court records to see if the names of all their respondents were there. None of those who had been to court failed to say so in the interview, nor did anyone fail to describe the offense or offenses with which he was charged. In addition, few responses were seriously incorrect. That is, no one claimed that he had never been guilty of lawbreaking and no one admitted having committed all of the violations they had included in their questions. Therefore, Erickson and Empey concluded that the data supplied by the respondents were reliable. Having satisfied themselves on this point, the sociologists tabulated their findings.

Clearly, the number of violations which respondents admitted having committed was tremendous (Table 1). The first two columns of Table 1 deal with the total volume of reported delinquency. In these columns types of offenses are ranked according to the totals for each type reported by *all four* groups of boys.

Analysis of Table 1 in terms of the questions originally raised by the sociologists reveals some interesting and often startling facts about juvenile delinquency. First, even casual examination of the data reveals the extraordinary number of violations committed by the 180 boys in the total sample. Three types of offenses were most common: theft, including shoplifting (24,199); especially of articles worth less than $2 (15,175); the purchase and drinking of alcohol (21,698); and offenses against property (12,278).

Second, when respondents were asked to tell whether anyone—parents, police, or others—had caught them committing various offenses, they admitted that more than nine out of ten offenses were undiscovered and unacted upon. This was especially true of the minor violations, such as theft of articles worth less than $50, buying and drinking liquor, and destroying property.

As might be expected, the picture changes with respect to more serious offenses such as the theft of more valuable property, breaking and entering, and arson. Fewer of these acts went unnoticed and unacted upon. But even in these cases, eight out of ten reported violations were not discovered, and nine out of ten violations did not lead to court action. Narcotics offenses, which were very few, but which are handled by the federal government and are the most serious of all, were never discovered or acted upon.

Third, comparison of Table 1 and Table 2 reveals the importance of distinguishing between the *frequency* with which a particular offense is committed by the four groups of youths and the *proportion* of each sample which admits having committed that delinquent act. For example, although roughly equal proportions of all four subsamples admitted to having engaged in theft of articles worth less than $2 (Table 2, top line), comparison of the *numbers* of thefts performed by the four groups (Table 1) shows important differences. If, for purposes of analysis, one combines the second two subsamples (those who offended repeatedly) and compares their total offenses with those of the first two groups (those who offended never, or only once), the violations of the repeated offenders—the recidivists—exceed those of the first two groups by thousands: thefts (excluding forgery, 20,836 compared with 2,851); offenses against property (10,828 compared with 1,450); offenses against the person (8,569 compared with 457); and the purchase and drinking of alcohol (21,134 compared with 564).

To find answers to their fourth question—Are the customary classifications of delinquents in delinquent and nondelinquent or institutionalized (in jail or reformatory) and noninstitutionalized based on real differences in behavior?—the sociologists examined their data from three viewpoints.

First, in comparing the subsample of 50 high school boys *with no previous court record* and the subsample of 30 *one-time offenders,* Erickson and Empey found that there was only one significant difference between the two groups: those officially labeled as offenders were more likely to have been involved in the destruction of property than the undiscovered delinquents, 84 percent as compared with 66 percent (Table 2). This did not im-

TABLE 2
Proportion of Respondents Committing Offenses

OFFENSE	RANK	PERCENT OF TOTAL	SUBSAMPLES			
			(1) 50 NON-DELINQUENTS	(2) 50 ONE-TIME OFFENDERS *	(3) 50 DELINQUENTS IN THE COMMUNITY	(4) 50 DELINQUENTS INCARCERATED
THEFT:	1					
Less than $2		93%	92%	98%	96%	86%
Worth $2 to $50		59	22	36	78	90
More than $50		26	2	2	46	54
Auto theft		29	2	2	54	60
Forgery		13	0	0	16	34
TRAFFIC OFFENSES:	2					
Driving without license		84	72	78	94	92
OFFENSES AGAINST PROPERTY:	3					
Breaking and entering		59	32	46	74	84
Destroying property		80	66	84	86	84
Setting fires (arson)		6	2	2	0	8

TABLE 2 (continued)

Proportion of Respondents Committing Offenses

OFFENSE	RANK	PERCENT OF TOTAL	SUBSAMPLES			
			(1) 50 NON-DELINQUENTS	(2) 50 ONE-TIME OFFENDERS *	(3) 50 DELINQUENTS IN THE COMMUNITY	(4) 50 DELINQUENTS INCARCERATED
OFFENSES CONCERNING ALCOHOL AND NARCOTICS:	4					
Buying beer or liquor		29	4	8	46	58
Drinking beer or liquor		74	52	66	84	94
Selling narcotics		0	0	0	0	2
Using narcotics		4	0	0	2	12
OFFENSES AGAINST THE PERSON:	5					
Armed robbery		5	0	0	4	14
Fighting, assault		70	52	60	82	86

* As explained in Table 1, the real total, 30, was multiplied by two-fifths to bring it up to 50, so this group could be compared with the other three groups.

press the sociologists as sufficient to justify the common habit of contrasting the delinquent with no court record with the one-time offender; except for this one violation, the two classes appeared, generally speaking, to commit the same offenses.

The second comparison was between one-time offenders and the subsample of 50 boys who were persistent but still not jailed offenders, that is, between the second and the third subsamples. Differences between these two groups on most offenses were marked. As a group, the persistent offenders were significantly—that is, 99 times out of 100—more inclined than one-time offenders, as a group, to have: stolen expensive and inexpensive items (many of these were shoplifted), bought and drunk liquor, stolen autos, fought, and driven without a license. There was also a clear difference with regard to forgery. Thus the conventional distinction between one-time and persistent offenders in the community was found to reflect, generally speaking, a true division.

The third and final comparison had to do with the noninstitutionalized (Subsample 3) versus the institutionalized offender (Subsample 4). Interestingly, although there were marked differences between the activities of the boys in the reformatory and the first two subsamples, there was very little between the kind and frequency of offenses committed by the incarcerated youths (Subsample 4) and those who were free but were persistent offenders (Subsample 3). Thus, the sociologists' findings seemed to indicate that of the various bases for comparison between delinquent groups, *persistence* (recidivism) is the most significant.

The sociologists' fifth question—that of the reliability of court records as an indication of delinquency—was not easy to answer. After exhaustive analysis of the data collected from their sample, Erickson and Empey concluded that official records are a more accurate reflection of an individual's single most serious violation than of the pattern of offenses, whether serious or not, which he most commonly commits. Further, it was clear to the sociologists that additional data on undetected offenses were needed if authorities were to plan realistic and effective measures to discourage delinquent behavior.

Thus, neither Mr. Chambers nor the police nor anyone else can depend upon official records for a true picture of how much delinquent behavior is going on in their communities, for so much of it is never discovered and so is never included in the reports of police and courts. Further, the research of Erickson and Empey suggests that comparisons such as those made between boys who have never been to court and those who have been to court once, rely on an overgeneralized classification and not on significant differences in types of adolescent behavior.

An interesting conclusion is justified by the findings on undetected delinquency, that is that if even a small fraction of it were, for some reason, to be suddenly disclosed and counted in the official records, there would appear to be a great wave of increased juvenile delinquency (without any significant change in actual delinquent behavior).

Three years after they had completed this research, the two Utah sociologists went over their data again, this time in order to discover if a boy's delinquencies were correlated with the social status of his family. The research team defined a family's social class by one of the several methods used by sociologists, namely, by the father's occupation. For convenience they classified occupations as upper (professional men and several classes of businessmen, scientists, and artists), middle (skilled and white-collar workers, including proprietors of small businesses), and lower (unskilled and semiskilled workers). Following this they sorted the boys of their sample into upper, middle, or lower status. Then they looked at their data on the boys' delinquencies —and found virtually no difference in the amount of delinquency attributed to the three status categories (Table 3). This fact is in strong contrast to the results the sociologists reached in their earlier research, when they compared the *officially* delinquent boys with those who were officially *not* delinquent.

However, when the sociologists made detailed comparisons of the *kinds* of delinquencies admitted by the youths in the three status groups, some interesting correlations came to light. For example: the upper-status group, although it contained 16 percent of the total number of boys, was guilty of only 9 percent of the total violations. Even the boys of upper status who were on probation or were incarcerated (Subsamples 3 and 4) made a better showing than those in the middle or lower status classes, for though these upper-status boys made up 9 percent of Subsample

TABLE 3 *
Distribution of Offenders by Offense and by Social Class

OFFENSE	UPPER (16 Percent of Sample) Violations	MIDDLE (55 Percent of Sample) Violations	LOWER (29 Percent of Sample) Violations
TRAFFIC Driving without a license	4%	51%	44%
THEFT			
Articles less than $2	10	61	29
Articles $2 to $50	5	69	26
Articles more than $50	8	59	33
Auto theft	2	60	38
Forgery	1	90	9
ALCOHOL AND NARCOTICS			
Buying alcohol	5	37	58
Drinking alcohol	8	59	33
Using narcotics	0	36	64

TABLE 3 * (continued)

Distribution of Offenders by Offense and by Social Class

OFFENSE	UPPER (16 PERCENT OF SAMPLE)	MIDDLE (55 PERCENT OF SAMPLE)	LOWER (29 PERCENT OF SAMPLE)
	VIOLATIONS	VIOLATIONS	VIOLATIONS
PROPERTY VIOLATIONS			
Breaking and entering	8	67	24
Destroying property	8	70	22
Arson	5	85	10
OFFENSES AGAINST PERSON			
Fighting and assault	2	45	52
Armed robbery	0	88	12

* Because of independent rounding of figures, percentages do not always total 100 percent.

3 and, again, 9 percent of Subsample 4, they confessed to only 6 percent of the offenses of the two subsamples.

If the upper-status boys were 16 percent of the total sample but contributed only 9 percent of the total violations, the other two status categories naturally must account for a disproportionate volume of the delinquent behavior. That is exactly what the research team discovered. Thus the middle-status category (55 percent of all the boys) admitted to 59 percent of the delinquencies. And the lower-status group (29 percent of the total sample) totaled 32 percent of the delinquencies.

Each status seems, as it were, to specialize. In contrast to the upper-status boys, those in the middle category contributed a disproportionate amount of theft and forgery, destruction of property, arson, and armed robbery. They committed in fact over two-thirds of the more serious violations. To pin it down more precisely: the boys of the middle status in Subsamples 3 and 4 accounted for a disproportionately large amount of the more serious delinquencies, so that Empey and Erickson conclude that the whole group of middle-status boys cannot be blamed for the excess of serious delinquency, but rather this "hard core."

Lower-status delinquents (29 percent of the sample) contributed proportions greater than 29 percent of the following violations: driving without a license and car theft, stealing articles worth more than $50, offenses involving alcohol or narcotics, and fighting.

Turning to the data on the boys of the three status classes, classified into the four subsamples and giving special attention to Subsamples 3 and 4 (those on parole and those incarcerated), Empey and Erickson found clear evidence that the most delinquent group of all was that of the boys of middle status in Subsamples 3 and 4.

Empey and Erickson feel safe in taking it for granted that 180 city boys would account for a greater volume of hidden delinquency than the 180 Mormon boys did. But until facts about undetected delinquency have been collected from samples of city youths, it is not possible to say positively that their *patterns* of delinquency are alike. Meanwhile this research has brought new knowledge of the extent of delinquency and some facts about what offenses are most likely to go undiscovered.

The Candidate
for Delinquency*

Is the explanation of delinquent gangs always that the boys feel deprived of social or economic advantages which other boys enjoy?

If a gang is **not** disadvantaged then what can explain its behavior?

Why do some members of the gang give up delinquent behavior?

The playground was dark as 15 boys slid quickly through the gate. Silently, a tall, husky boy with "Dukes" written across the back of his jacket held up his hand and motioned to the others to stop. Then the leader carefully unbuckled his belt and slipped it off, letting the sharpened buckle swing free. The others, also wearing Duke emblems, took off their belts, too, and one youth flicked open a switchblade.

"Click!" The Dukes froze as they heard a sound by the far corner of the park. "CLICK!" "CLICK!" Now reflection from the streetlight glinted off steel knife blades snapped open by yet unseen hands.

Suddenly, 20 boys flung themselves from the shadows on the invading Dukes. Weapons and fists hit leather-jacketed bodies. But then the sound of approaching police cars was heard. Both gangs fled from the oncoming sirens and the fight was over as quickly as it had begun. When the squad cars arrived, they found the playground deserted except for a heavy leather belt with a razor sharp buckle and a badly ripped Duke jacket—mute evidence of the vicious struggle which had just ended.

As the police checked the park, one of the young officers questioned his partner about the gangs. Why, he asked, did boys join groups like the Dukes when they knew the danger of con-

* Adapted from "The Uncommitted Adolescent: Candidate for Gang Socialization" by Larry Karacki and Jackson Toby. Originally published in *Sociological Inquiry*, Vol. 32, No. 2 (1962), pp. 203–215. Reprinted in revised form by permission of the Editor, *Sociological Inquiry*.

stant fighting? Why didn't they get jobs or go in for sports instead of stealing everything in sight and spending hours drinking beer and playing cards? Why were they always truant from school when everyone realized that you had to have a high school diploma? The older policeman, like most people, was unable to give his troubled helper any easy answers.

Puzzling over the same questions and realizing the importance of the problem, sociologists Larry Karacki and Jackson Toby focused their attention on the Dukes, hoping to find out why these particular boys formed a delinquent gang.

The Dukes were not deprived of ordinary advantages, and so could not be explained in the way some sociologists explain gangs—as groups of boys who suffer from the lack of things which they see other people enjoying. Then what was the explanation? During the summer of 1960, Larry Karacki moved to the large Midwestern city in which the Dukes lived and took a room in a small boardinghouse near their hangout, to learn *why* they were delinquent.

The Dukes had been organized in the summer of 1955, ostensibly for the purpose of having parties. The 20 original members elected officers and established a treasury, naming the club "The Mafia" at the insistence of the president. Not surprisingly, several parents insisted that the name be changed, and the gang settled on "The Dukes."

In spite of its supposedly social nature, from 1955 to 1958 the gang was chiefly engaged in delinquent activities. Some members who had a history of delinquency joined the group in order to continue their deviant behavior. Other boys committed their first offenses after joining the Dukes. Starting with petty theft, the Dukes quickly widened their range of delinquent activities to include grand larceny, armed robbery, sexual promiscuity, rape, and numerous minor violations.

Despite this diversity of offenses which seemed to stop only at drug-using, the Dukes were primarily concerned with street brawls. Proud of a deserved reputation for being the toughest gang in town, they accorded the highest positions of esteem and leadership to their best fighters.

However, the gang was not completely free of the norms and criticism of their families and neighborhood. The boys rationalized their fighting as self-defense, maintaining that they had never started a fight. They explained their encounters with rival gangs by describing their opponents as "punks" or "wise guys" who, unlike the Dukes, did not realize that fighting was "stupid." Thus, the Dukes took pride in their "rep" (reputation) as a fighting gang and, while denying they sought it, they considered their fame a just and fitting reward for teaching their rivals a lesson.

The gang's fights ranged from impromptu scuffles involving one or two Dukes to well-planned "rumbles" in which almost all the boys took part. Many of their brawls were at Hamilton Park (their "turf"), but fights also occurred at schools, taverns, restaurants, parties, and on the streets. The number of their battles was considerable and no doubt contributed to their reputation for violence. But more important was the brutal, almost savage behavior of the Dukes during a fight. On one occasion a Duke hospitalized two opponents with a blow from behind with an aluminum crutch. At another time, a Duke had to be forcibly removed while stomping on a boy who as a result had to spend several weeks in the hospital. Yet all the Dukes claimed that they "had never started a fight"!

By 1960, when the two sociologists began their study of the Dukes, the gang had begun to change back into a social club. Of the 33 members, most had reached the age of 18 or over, a point at which gangs are likely to disintegrate spontaneously. Further, the City Recreation Department had assigned a part-time worker to the group, and the members engaged in informal athletic events and held dances fairly regularly. This shift to more conventional activities split the Dukes into two cliques: (1) those who had no further interest in delinquency, and (2) those who continued to fight and steal. But in spite of these later developments, the sociologists knew that the Dukes had been a delinquent gang, and they turned their attention to possible reasons for its original formation.

First, had the boys who joined the Dukes been deprived in a socioeconomic sense? Karacki and Toby discovered that, on the contrary, most of the Dukes' parents were homeowners who had lived in Hamilton Park for years and whose occupations put them in the upper-working-class or the lower-middle-class. Hamilton Park itself was far from a slum area, a fact supported by a mass of data provided by the 1950 Census (Table 1). Therefore, it was

TABLE 1

Characteristics of Hamilton Park and of the City

	HAMILTON PARK	TOTAL CITY
A. *Population Characteristics* *		
White	100	84
Nonwhite	—	16
Living in complete families	92	76
Median school years completed . . .	9	9
Income of $5,000 or more	34	18
Median income	$4,237	$3,153
Males unemployed	3	6
Occupation of male employed: †		
Professional, technical and kindred	8	6
Managers, officials, and proprietors	9	8
Clerical and kindred	12	9
Sales workers	7	5
Craftsmen, foremen, and kindred	31	24
Operatives and kindred	21	28
Service workers	6	7
Laborers	5	10
B. *Housing Characteristics*		
Owner occupied	75	42
Median value	$11,974	$10,027
No private bath or dilapidated . . .	1	14
Year built:		
1930 or later	17	11

* Unless otherwise specified, figures are given as percentages.
† Because of independent rounding of figures, percentages do not total 100 percent.

clear that the socioeconomic background of the Dukes was at least average and often higher.

Second, were the boys members of a disadvantaged racial group which was predisposed to failure because of prejudice and discrimination? Here again, the sociologists ran into a stone wall. Although there was a substantial black minority in the city, there were no black members in the gang.

A third possibility: were the individuals who became Dukes frustrated by some major handicaps which would hinder their participation in the educational and occupational life of the community? The two sociologists found that while the Dukes performed poorly as students and employees, there was considerable evidence that they were *unwilling*, not *unable*, to devote themselves to school or work. Vocational and aptitude tests showed that most of the members had performed far below their potentialities.

Karacki and Toby saw more direct evidence in the adjustments being made by those Dukes who, in 1960, were in the process of "settling down." A number of the boys returned to school, either to finish high school or to begin college. In several instances, they had paid for resuming their education by steady employment. To others, jobs were ends in themselves rather than means for financing further schooling. But not all Dukes had made nondelinquent adjustments at the time the sociologists conducted their study (Table 2). However, as of April 1961, it was clear that most of the gang had acquired something they had conspicuously lacked earlier: the motivation to achieve along conventional lines.

Having realized that the "deprivation theory" and their other ideas could not explain the Dukes' behavior, Karacki and Toby probed yet another hypothesis: namely, that lack of commitment to the adult way of life was at the root of the problem. Using the concept of "youth culture" with its emphasis on irresponsibility, the pursuit of pleasure, and expressive behavior, the sociologists formed the impression that the Dukes had failed to develop early in adolescence that commitment to adult roles and values which would have served to relate the boys to school and work. Lacking, then, direction for their energies and interests, they drew upon the youth culture for meaning and purpose. Out of this emerged a delinquent gang.

Karacki and Toby found evidence for their theory in the fact that much of the delinquent behavior of the Dukes had been an expression of three values of the youth culture: (1) desire for im-

TABLE 2

Occupations and Delinquency Record of the Dukes

Continued Delinquents:

1. Edward M.: Now in Army.
2. Henry G.: Recent inductee into Army after year as part-time handy man for city.
3. Roger M.: Unemployed nearly two years; recent Army inductee.
4. Ronald M.: Unemployed nearly two years.
5. Kenneth Y.: Completing trade school, one year behind class.
6. William C.: Completing day high school, one year behind class.
7. Terrance M.: Employed part time as a wall washer.
8. Richard S.: Employed at government motor pool, seventh job in past year.
9. Melvin L.: Drop out from college, now unemployed.
10. Donald L.: Plumber's apprentice for past six months.

Doubtful If Still Delinquents:

1. Robert D.: In Army.
2. Gerald K.: In Army.
3. James B.: Completing first year of college.
4. Harold W.: Completing second year of college.

Nondelinquents:

1. William A.: In Army.
2. John L.: In Army.
3. John F.: Employed as machine operator; recent Army inductee.
4. Joseph G.: In Army, preparing to become an auto mechanic.
5. John A.: In Air Force, assigned to college physics research lab.
6. Carmon C.: Recently returned from Army; formerly head copy boy for a local newspaper.
7. William H.: In Army, attending night school to obtain high school diploma.
8. Robert J.: Unemployed, attending night school to obtain high school diploma.
9. David S.: Salesman in children's store.
10. Gerald C.: Head chef at local outlet of a national restaurant chain.
11. Gerald O.: Near completion of plumber's apprenticeship.
12. Frank L.: Truck driver-handy man for plumbing concern, attending night school to obtain high school diploma; plans to go to college.
13. Neil L.: Machine operator, attending night school to obtain high school diploma; plans to go to college.
14. Joseph D.: Milkman, attending night college.
15. Thomas H.: Full-time timekeeper plus part-time work, attending night college while saving to attend full time.
16. James C.: Full-time park employee; part-time cleaning a tavern; attends evening college; saving to attend full time.
17. John E.: Completing first year of college with B average.

mediate pleasure; (2) loyalty to peers; and (3) assertion of masculinity through physical aggression.

The Dukes' search for "kicks" was clearly revealed in their joy rides through the countryside, beer and wine parties, and occasional acts of vandalism. Hedonism, or the love of pleasure for its own sake, was also involved on those occasions when stealing became a game to see who could get away with the most. Although these thefts could be materially rewarding, the Dukes would tell how they abandoned stealing in favor of a party or some other diversion. Lack of "things to do" was their greatest complaint about the neighborhood.

The importance attached to peer loyalty by the gang was best seen in the explanation given by one of them of what "going all out for a guy" meant:

> If a guy called up and needed help, no matter when he was calling, you'd be willing to give help. Also, if he needed money, you would lend it, and if he was in a fight, you'd be willing to stand by him and get beat up if it meant that. You wouldn't let him down in a tight spot.

While immediate pleasure and gang loyalty were very important to all the Dukes, the assertion of masculinity through physical aggression was perhaps the value they appreciated most highly. Their best and most active fighters were boxers and weight lifters, and members who were "tough guys" were likely to enjoy high status among them.

The sociologists found further support for their theory when they examined the shift of many of the Dukes to nondelinquent behavior. It appeared that the nondelinquents tended to be boys who had changed from the youth culture to adult roles and norms and who had successfully returned to school or work. (See Table 2.)

In contrast, Dukes who in 1960 were still involved in brawls and thefts showed no sign of an adjustment in orientation. These boys still clung to the youth culture: they continued to be weight lifters, boxers, "lovers," "agitators," and "tough guys," seeking thrills in their fights with rival gangs in the park at night.

After their study of the Dukes was completed, Karacki and Toby realized that their data raised general questions about the theory of deprivation as an explanation of the formation of adolescent gangs. Might it be, the sociologists wondered, that the relationship between socioeconomic deprivation and adolescent alienation has been misunderstood? In the light of their experience with the Dukes, Karacki and Toby concluded that it is actually the lack of commitment to school and other approved and conventional institutions which makes gang membership attractive. Thus the Dukes probably shared one important characteristic with adolescent boys in a deprived environment who turned to delinquent gangs—a lack of belief in and commitment to the roles and values of the adult world.

The Slum: Opportunities for
Crime and Delinquency*

Are the social and economic opportunities offered to young people the same in all slums?

If not, how do these opportunities differ, as between one slum and another?

Do particular kinds of delinquents seem to belong in particular kinds of slums?

In which kind of slum are the delinquents most likely to a) take drugs? b) enter criminal careers? c) belong in fighting gangs?

Tony Santella's neighborhood was a slum. The people there, including Tony's parents, were uneducated, poor, and employed in menial jobs.

Tony was shrewder than his parents and more ambitious. After school, he tried to make money by shining shoes downtown and doing odd jobs for neighborhood shopkeepers. It was on the first occasion that he was hired to sweep the floor of a cigar store near his home that he encountered Harry Wisoski.

Harry Wisoski was a familiar name to the boys of the neighborhood because Harry himself had been a neighborhood boy who graduated to a half-secret life of shiny cars, sharp clothes, and plenty of money. Exactly how Harry had come by these things was never positively stated; but everyone understood that his success was connected with the automatic that he carried.

When Tony's employer hailed Harry as he entered the cigar store, Tony stopped sweeping and stared. Then he started sweeping furiously. "Hey, kid," Harry said. "How 'bout wiping off my car?"

* Adapted from Chapter 7, *Delinquency and Opportunity* by Richard A. Cloward and Lloyd E. Ohlin (New York: The Free Press, 1960). Reprinted by permission.

Tony was thrilled. And he was barely able to say thanks when Harry gave him a dollar for his work.

Partly because Tony had swept well and partly because the store owner had also been impressed by Harry's tip, Tony became the regular sweeper in the store from then on. He saw Harry frequently and on each occasion Harry gave him a job to do and chatted with him. Tony's awe and admiration soared, and he resolved to follow in Harry's footsteps.

Harry stopped visiting the neighborhood some time after that, but by then his friendliness toward Tony had been noted by the other neighborhood boys; and on the strength of that, Tony was invited into the gang that made its headquarters on the corner just south of his home. He was flattered, because most of the gang members were a year older than he; and to prove his merit he began making up dramatic stories about Harry's exploits. He also started to push and pummel and pick fights with enthusiasm. Within a few months, he knew his place in the gang was secure.

The gang, however, felt anything but secure. One day, when the boys were chasing happily through the neighborhood, they forgot themselves and ran through an adjoining neighborhood. The next day the gang from the invaded territory returned the visit and beat Tony and his friends to their knees. To strengthen its position, the shattered gang began to make overtures to an older neighborhood gang called the Tigers.

The Tigers had an established reputation for toughness. They were also known to be accomplished car thieves. The boys were 16 or 17 years old; but the real boss of the gang, who was rarely seen on the streets with the others, was 25. His name was Lonnie.

Tony's gang realized that the Tigers, under ordinary circumstances, would have nothing to do with them; but they hoped to win acceptance on the strength of the fact that Lonnie and the other Tigers were neighborhood boys, too. Some, in fact, were their own brothers. But to their dismay they were rebuffed, and it was all too obvious why: they were inexperienced, ineffective weaklings. They set out to prove themselves otherwise.

All the members of Tony's gang had always done a certain amount of casual shoplifting and stealing from cars parked in the streets. Now they went about the work systematically. Their single aim was to gain experience and prove themselves experts. Though poor, they were not at first interested in any possible gain from what they stole; and they casually disposed of most of their loot in dark alleys and the river. But soon realizing that such waste was foolish, they established working arrangements with one of the neighborhood "fences," who offered suggestions about how they could make money from their work.

Gradually their exploits began to win the Tigers' approval. Finally, the day came when one of Lonnie's lieutenants told them that if they would like to come along, the Tigers could use two of them to help size up a job that was being considered.

Tony was one of the boys selected because Harry Wisoski had once mentioned him favorably to Lonnie. Since he took pains to carry his modest assignment out well, Tony was given a second chance to work with the Tigers. And again he did well. But then he did not hear from the older gang for eight weeks.

Fearing he had flunked his test, Tony made his first immature but understandable mistake: to demonstrate his worthiness, he overacted his criminal role. He provoked a bloody fight between his gang and one from a riverfront neighborhood. He needlessly beat up one of his own neighborhood's elderly derelicts. And unaware that his former cigar-store employer was a bookie connected with the city's syndicate, he broke in and ransacked the store.

Having seen boys act in this way before, the Tigers were understanding but displeased. They saw promise in Tony, but like all businesslike gangs, they had no use for purposeless, untrammeled behavior. So the message they delivered to Tony was clear and brief: "Knock it off, punk!"

Tony obeyed almost to the point of overacting in the opposite way. But it was a year before the Tigers gave him another assignment and two years before they admitted him as a provisional member. Then he spent another year developing the art of breaking into stores protected by burglar alarms before he gained full membership. From then on, he rose steadily in organized crime in the city.

While young people in all walks of life may turn into juvenile delinquents, the great majority of delinquents grow up in the slums. But why do some slum youths become professional criminals like Tony Santella while others are nothing more than hooligans and still others wind up as drug addicts or alcoholics? And, of course, there is one more question: why is it that most slum boys are *not* delinquent? An early survey of delinquency showed that in the worst districts in Chicago only 19 out of every 100 boys between 10 to 16 years of age were taken to the juvenile court.*

The answers, according to Richard A. Cloward and Lloyd E. Ohlin, sociologists at the New York School of Social Work at Columbia University, lie in the kind of slum in which they grow up. As a research team the two sociologists drew upon studies made by others and on their own extensive work, which includes studies of gangs in Chicago and work on parole boards and on government commissions. The theories presented below are the fruits of reflection upon their experience.

The slum that produces professional criminals is characterized by the close knitting together of the lives and activities of the people in the community. For one thing, boys are more or less constantly exposed to neighborhood teen-agers who are in the process of becoming criminals and to men who have become neighborhood heroes as professional criminals. Inspired by the success of these older people, the boys set out to follow their example. This is flattering to the men; and because they can always make use of additional manpower to expand their operations, they see to it that the boys are trained in criminal ways and given ample opportunity to demonstrate their skills. Despite this display of interest, however, the boys are always made to feel that they are on trial; so, for example, they often steal more things than they can use simply to acquire a skill that will improve their standing in the eyes of the organization. They also frequently show off by engaging in an extraordinary number of exploits, outdoing more experienced lawbreaking criminals. This usually earns them a reprimand, because organized crime is a business and does not tolerate members who act in an undisciplined, unbusinesslike way.

* See "Delinquency Areas" in *Cities and City Life* in this *Readings in Sociology* Series.

In a slum that produces criminals, there is also close cooperation between criminals and youths who aspire to crime on one hand and semilegitimate businessmen on the other. Such men include fences, junk dealers, lawyers, bail bondsmen, fixers, crooked police officers, and the like. Unless a budding criminal can establish good working relations with these men, he has little chance to work into a stable, protected criminal career.

Since in the slum that nurtures professional criminals the various elements work together and depend upon each other, Cloward and Ohlin speak of it as "integrated." A second type, slums that produce uncontrolled rowdies, or hooligans, are, by contrast, almost totally without this sort of integration and cohesiveness. The local young delinquents do not form connections with locally established criminals because the neighborhood's population is constantly changing. Such slums may contain huge housing projects which are populated, not by long-time residents, but by newcomers from other areas. Or the long-time residents may have left when industry moved in. Cloward and Ohlin explain that in a slum made unstable because its residents are highly mobile and transient, tentative efforts at integration of people of various ages and occupations do not succeed. An unorganized community such as this does not provide an easy way for young people to get into legitimate enterprise and they grow discontented and frustrated. It may be just as hard for them to get into the stable criminal world because the unstable community does not provide the established connections between individuals and such institutions as pawn shops and "fences" which are needed by organized crime. The young, in short, being deprived of both conventional and criminal opportunities, grow angry. And since social controls in the unintegrated slum are weak, irrational violence goes unchecked, and to excel in violent behavior becomes the only route by which young men can gain a reputation, or, as they say, "rep."

The story of Henny Jones illustrates what often happens to boys who live in chaotic, unintegrated slums.

Henny did not know his father or even who he was. He lived with his mother, two sisters, and a younger brother. They were a shiftless family. In the first 10 years of Henny's life, they occupied seven different flats in seven different neighborhoods in the city. They were forced to move, once by the urban renewal agency. On the other occasions, they moved either to cut their rent or to get larger quarters.

When he was 10, Henny went to Public School No. 36. It was a big, dingy building of granite blocks surrounded by a six-foot fence of rusty iron. The windows were covered with heavy steel mesh to ward off bricks and bottles. The playground was continually littered with glass and was often adorned with old automobile tires and fenders.

Henny was in the fifth grade but was able to read only at the third-grade level—and just barely at that. Although his teachers regularly stressed reading and gave more time to it than any other subjects, Henny had attended too many overcrowded schools to get the kind of help he needed.

Public School No. 36 was in a neighborhood populated mainly by blacks and Puerto Ricans who had moved just as often as the Jones family. In the morning when Henny and other neighborhood children walked to school they passed only a few adults who were traveling to work.

After school, Henny and his friends played on the streets until dark. They chased one another; played stickball; tried to turn on fire hydrants; threw objects at passing cars; smashed bottles; stole food, candy, and anything they could from street vendors and stores; fought; jumped on smaller children; and screamed constantly. Their existence was aimless, useless and, if they ever sat down quietly to think about it, unhappy.

It never occurred to Henny to do something that would earn money because he knew almost no one who worked. But even if he had decided to make the effort, he could not have gone far because the neighborhood shopkeepers wanted to have nothing to do with Public School No. 36 children, and he did not have the money to buy even the little equipment needed to shine shoes.

Early opportunity to enter the world of organized crime, as Tony Santella did, was denied Henny. The Mafia and other notorious criminal bands steered clear of the area. This does not mean, however, that Henny was not exposed to crime. He saw a great deal of it, but it was unsystematic, unprofessional, and "small time." The father of one of Henny's friends, for instance, was a pickpocket who was so unskilled at the work of picking pockets that he was never out of prison for more than a few months in a year. Another was caught holding up a gas station.

Henny himself stole whenever opportunity offered; and when he was thirteen, he was taken into a gang called the Sinners, which for a time made a specialty of shoplifting. But this pastime was forgotten when another neighborhood gang—the Raiders—provoked a rumble. The Sinners did not do well in the battle; and when they had finished licking their wounds, they vowed revenge. Almost constant warfare between the groups ensued.

Eventually, violence reached such a point that the city welfare department felt compelled to assign a social worker to the Sinners. "Hey, you must think we're pretty bad!" Henny remarked to the man, whose name was Rogers. Henny's voice was full of pride; and Rogers instantly recognized that it would be unwise to confirm the comment. But Henny and the other Sinners could not be fooled. They knew that Rogers would not be spending so much time with them if the city authorities were not upset by their exploits, and they felt honored. Deep down, they also felt that to have Rogers assigned to them meant they were no longer outcasts. On the contrary, the world which had ignored them had at last decided to help them. And because of this, they grew less violent and began to enjoy the program Rogers set up.

The Raiders, however, were jealous. So were several other nearby gangs. They felt that Rogers' assignment to the Sinners was not only an honor for the Sinners but also a sign of disrespect toward themselves. It meant they had not been so troublesome as the Sinners. So they tried to take revenge on the Sinners —and indirectly on the city—by launching a new, all-out attack on them.

This was too much for the Sinners. Much as they liked Rogers, his program and the new reputation his presence had given them, they could not allow their rivals to walk over them. So, having survived the Raiders' latest aggression, they retaliated with an even fiercer attack.

Two boys were killed. One was a Raider. The other was Henny. He was surrounded by flames when a bullet crashed through the gas tank of a car behind which he was crouching.

No one could come near enough, in the terrible heat, to rescue the screaming boy.

There is a third type of reaction to the slum, one depending very much on the youth's personality. There will be some boys who "do not make it" as criminals. Yet the slum offers them very little opportunity to engage in a well-respected career. They are thus double failures.

Some double failures sink into the milder forms of delinquency of the "corner boys." As they grow older, jobs and marriage and family responsibilities hold them in control. They outgrow the corner gang.

But others find another solution: they retreat from reality. Retreatism is achieved by alcohol or drugs which take the youth away from his troubles for a time and carry him into a world where he can see himself as an important being or into a world of pure fantasy and dreams.

One theory is that drug addicts and alcoholics try to avoid facing up to life because they are unable to achieve a legitimate, socially accepted goal and yet they cannot bring themselves to strive for an unlawful, unacceptable goal. From their observations of delinquency among slum youth, however, Cloward and Ohlin concluded that this explanation did not, in most cases, fit the facts. Indeed, they found that most lower-class drug addicts are delinquents before they start taking drugs regularly. Obviously, then, they are not in doubt about what goal they want to achieve, but are already accustomed to lawbreaking.

Why then do slum youths take drugs in order to escape from reality? The two sociologists have a threefold answer: (1) Because they grow up in a neighborhood that is well peopled with addicts and "pushers" (drug sellers). After all, it is difficult to become interested in drugs if you are not exposed to people who use them and have them for sale. (2) Because the neighborhood —like all slum areas—affords little opportunity for the youths to get into legitimate enterprise. And (3) because the young fail to achieve standing either as professional criminals or to excel in undisciplined violence. To repeat, they are *double* failures.

Because it is a crime to buy, possess, or sell narcotic drugs, it is necessary for the drug-user to make secret connections with the sellers of drugs. The drug habit thus calls for a network of supplies, peddlers, and customers all of whom must be able to reach each other, out of sight of the public and of the police. There must then be, to some extent, a local integration of people and institutions, just as in the slum in which professional criminals thrive. But beyond that, the drug addict usually pursues his habit in private. He retreats from society into a world of fantasy and private experience * from which he emerges when the withdrawal sickness (which is the unfailing sign that the habit has taken hold of him) drives him back into the world of "connections," or "pushers," to secure a new supply of narcotics. And because the drug traffic is illegal, this world to which he returns regularly is the criminal world.

Consider the case of Joe Wisehart. Joe is today a 19-year-old inmate of a state institution. He was put there because he had become addicted to narcotics.

Joe and his father, a drug addict, and his weak-willed, slovenly mother lived in a slum that offered ample opportunity for a boy to build a reputation as a delinquent. Joe, however, was not quite able to take advantage of it.

He tried, of course. He was insecure and looked down upon. But he was unusually big and strong for his age. One day when a member of the Buffo gang picked a fight with him for no particular reason except to show off, Joe pinned him down in a minute. The other Buffos promptly decided that Joe should replace the member he had defeated.

Joe worked hard to be a worthy member of the gang. He was not always successful with his fists, because some of the smaller boys were faster and tougher than he. But he made up for this by keeping the gang supplied with cigarettes which he stole from newsstands and cigar stores.

As Joe and his comrades grew older, however, he gradually lost his "rep." First, his physical growth stopped and instead of being one of the bigger boys, he found he was one of the smaller ones. This, coupled with his natural timidity, put him at a serious disadvantage when gang warfare broke out. In addition, many of the other Buffos became expert in more difficult forms

* See "Cats, Kicks, and Color" in *Cities and City Life* in this *Readings in Sociology* Series.

of crime, and they looked down on Joe's shoplifting as "baby stuff."

Although he knew he was on the downgrade in the gang's estimation, Joe did not realize to what depths he had actually fallen until one day, when the Buffos set out on a particularly dangerous mission, he was told to remain on the gang's street corner and keep watch for marauding neighborhood gangs. This was ordinarily a job given to one of the girls that were attached to the gang.

Lonely and humiliated, Joe had his first marijuana cigarette that night. He got it from a boy he knew who was often "high on pot." And the next day he avoided the corner where the gang had its hang-out. In the gang's eyes he was a failure and he could not face their scorn. In the evening when he felt depressed and rejected he began seeking out his friend, to get enough "pot" for a smoke which would carry him off to a dream world where the gang did not count. Weeks went by and Joe forgot the gang and lived for his dreams.

There came a day when he had no money for marijuana. On the impulse of the moment he snatched at a woman's purse. She held it tightly and her screams attracted the attention of a policeman.

Tony was charged with having marijuana in his possession and with robbery. He was 19 years old now and no longer belonged in the juvenile court. So he was lucky that the judge proved to be an understanding man who, instead of sentencing him for snatching the purse, or for having marijuana (the penalty for that is up to a year in prison), committed him for treatment to a state institution for addicts.

In summary: Cloward and Ohlin have described three delinquent subcultures, associated with two types of slums.

The criminal subculture belongs in the integrated slum, where a youth may launch upon a stable criminal career, encouraged and supported by the well-established conventional and criminal institutions.

The conflict subculture is found in the unintegrated slum. Here the criminal elements have not meshed with the conventional institutions and the young residents of the slum find support from neither of them. Lacking either approved or criminal opportunities, frustrated youths turn to violent behavior which the neighborhood makes no effective attempts to control.

Finally, the sociologists describe a personal reaction to slum conditions: retreatism. This is an escape from facing the hard fact that they have failed at entering a criminal career, held back, probably, by conscience, and at an honest career because no real opportunities in that direction are open to them.

Lower-Class Culture
and Delinquency*

What are some of the features of slum life which give rise to delinquent behavior?

What kinds of things are of special concern to residents of slums?

What is the role of gang membership in the lives of slum adolescents?

Do slum youth engage in crime primarily because they are angry at middle-class people?

The behavior of the gangs of corner boys who "hang," that is, meet, on street corners in slum districts of our cities has been studied by Dr. Walter B. Miller for many years. The account of gangs and of their major concerns which follows is based on his findings in the late 1950s. During this period rival gangs like those of **West Side Story** and certain "violent" gangs with their switchblade knives and their leather coats and big boots were making exciting newspaper, magazine, and film stories and television programs. More recently, groups such as the Black Panthers and black youth gangs, often with racist aims, have received a good deal of attention. But the behavior of corner boys is much the same today as Dr. Miller found it in the 1950s. It is simply that, at the moment, corner boys are losing their fascination for the public, as the news media focus more and more on the ghettos, adolescent crime, and organized protest in the schools and universities.

When he was 11 years old, William ("Cool Bill") Martin was arrested for shoplifting and when he was 12 for stealing a car. When he was 13, Cool Bill led a gang, the "Diamonds," and

---

* Adapted from "Lower Class Culture as a Generating Milieu of Gang Delinquency," by Walter B. Miller, *Journal of Social Issues*, Vol. 14, No. 3 (July 1958), pp. 5–19; also Chapter IV, *City Gangs* (John Wiley & Sons, forthcoming). Reprinted by permission.

at 14 he was suspended from school for extorting lunch money from younger and weaker children not in his gang. When he was 15, he was accused of fathering a child, but it was never proved. At 16, the legal dropout age, he left school although he was still in the eighth grade. And, from the time he left school until he got a "break" as a runner for the local numbers racketeer, Cool Bill hung around the corner and supported himself by petty thievery and by "rolling" (robbing) drunks.

To the police, teachers, probation officers, welfare workers, and the courts, Cool Bill Martin was a born troublemaker—a blight on society, an outcast, an obstinate, stupid, cruel, amoral, and destructive person destined to a life of crime. But to members of the Diamonds, other street-corner friends, and even some of the adult criminals of the neighborhood, he was a minor hero —"a smart kid," a fellow who could take care of himself, "one of the crowd." Obviously Cool Bill could be two completely different people—depending on whether he is judged by the standards of teachers, police, and welfare workers, or by the values of drug addicts, numbers players, bookies, dropouts, and street-corner kids.

Can values be so different that a boy is a bum in one community and a hero in another? The answer is *yes.* Dr. Walter B. Miller, who studies the causes of juvenile delinquency, reports that many so-called delinquent acts of slum youths actually may be attempts to win rewards and respect in their own special society. When Cool Bill violates laws and moral standards, he is really upholding many traditions, patterns, and beliefs of life as he knows it. He and the thousands of youngsters like him who seem to be in conflict with their community are really *conformists* to values transmitted by centuries of slum culture.

To discover these values, Dr. Miller launched upon three years of study, during which his research staff kept in close contact with 21 street-corner gangs in the slum district of an eastern city. At the conclusion of the investigation, he was able to spell out some of the important values of the "corner boys." His report is presented here. In the years since Dr. Miller wrote it, it has become a classic work in criminology, widely quoted by the experts.

VALUES AND SLUM LIFE

A slum neighborhood is easy to recognize by, for one thing, its large number of female-dominated households, that is, homes where the fathers are absent, dead, missing, or unknown. Another distinctive feature is that marriages there are frequent and short-lived and in many households the couple may not be actually married. Most important, those lower-class families who are the long-time residents of the slum hold certain important beliefs, or concepts, about life that differ significantly from those of the middle class.* They have a culture of their own and that culture is one with a long history. Dr. Miller discovered the following values, or "focal concerns" in the slum culture:

TROUBLE

Getting into trouble and staying out of trouble are major concerns. For men, "trouble" usually involves drinking, fighting, or misadventures with women. For women, trouble means casual affairs with men and the problems they associate with the other sex. But to the residents of the slum the issue of whether their trouble is legally or morally wrong is often less important to them than staying out of trouble that can cause consequences such as arrest, disease, injury, or unwanted family responsibilities.

In the slum a man is judged not by achievements or accomplishments but by his "trouble potential." A slum mother frequently approves her daughter's choice of a boyfriend not on the basis of his family background or education or earning power but on his ability to stay out of trouble.

In some situations, getting into trouble actually brings a certain prestige, especially among criminals and youthful gang members. And, if trouble does not always bring prestige, at least it is often recognized as the fastest means to other ends, such as thrills, or easy income, or free welfare aid.

Of course, the individual in the slum still must make a choice between lawbreaking and law-abiding behavior. Indeed, it is not uncommon for a single family to produce one son who is a criminal and another who is a policeman.

---

* See "The Slum: Who Has to Live There and Who Chooses to Live There?" in *Cities and City Life* in this *Readings in Sociology* Series.

TOUGHNESS

The concern of men in the slum with "toughness" is almost legendary. Lower-class men, whether slum dwellers or not, make constant demonstrations of their physical strength and athletic skill; they may proclaim their masculinity by tattooing their bodies, or avoiding sentimentality, or scorning anything that smacks of art or literature; or by bravery in the face of physical threats. Of course, the models of the perfect "tough guy"—hard, fearless, unemotional, and skilled in hand-to-hand combat—can be seen any night on television in the gangster, the private-eye, and the cowboy shows.

Some sociologists argue that their admiration of toughness stems from the fact that many slum boys have been brought up in female-dominated households. Lacking fathers to teach them male roles realistically, they grow up obsessed with proving their masculinity. Perhaps for the same reason, a fear of homosexuality runs deep. For instance, anyone who shows refinement or "softness"—even a friend who tries to move out of the slum—may be ridiculed as a "queer."

Naturally, the concern over masculinity makes it difficult for these men openly to show affection for each other. Sentiments of loyalty, brotherhood, or friendship among members of street-corner gangs are disguised by aggressive "roughhousing," kidding, and name-calling. Such indirect ways of showing affection are often seen, however, in other all-male groups in other classes of society and other parts of the city. Fraternity boys, athletic team-mates, soldiers, or men in prisons act very much the same way as men hanging around the street corners of the slum.

SMARTNESS

For many people of low status, to be "smart" means to outsmart, outfox, outwit, dupe, "put on" or "con" others—and to remain "unconned" oneself! Smartness is the ability to achieve material goods and personal status through great quick-wittedness and little physical effort. In other words, the "smart guy can make a fast buck living by his wits."

This smartness is not learned in school; the school's type of intellectual development in literature, art, and "good" music is considered effeminate. Slum children learn smartness on the street corners, where they constantly practice the arts of duping and outfoxing others. Card games, gambling, and the exchange of insults may all be ways of trying to "con" each other. The razzing, the kidding, the "put-ons" often persist into later life. Adult black males, for example, often carry on stylized exchanges of verbal abuse, usually aiming their insults at each others' mothers. In these exchanges, the winner is the "smart guy" with the fastest and most imaginative "comebacks."

To many of the dwellers in the slum, the world is divided into two types of people: the squares who work for their money and deserve to be conned, and the hustlers who live by conning the "suckers," as they call their victims.

EXCITEMENT

To many slum people, life is a dull rhythm of routine and repetitive events spiced infrequently by brief moments of great emotional or physical stimulation. Indeed, a characteristic aspect of slum life is the search for excitement or thrills, often by way of drugs, alcohol, sex, or gambling.

For example, a common pastime is "goin' out on the town," or more simply, "bar-hoppin'." An individual, or a group, makes the rounds of the bars, drinking continually throughout the evening. Gambling, fights between men over women, or claims to physical prowess are all part of the night's fun. Since making the rounds has an almost certain promise of wild excitement, the individuals actually seem to be seeking out its dangers.

Many slum men and women seek out such adventures regularly, perhaps every Saturday night. In between times they may pay the price of these episodes of flirting with danger by nursing hangovers and bruises or spending time in jail or in paying fines. For many, much of their free time is spent doing nothing—just "hanging around" the corner, "shooting the breeze." This cycle of long periods of inactivity and short bursts of excitement may be as regular as clockwork.

FATE

Many people of low status believe that their lives are controlled by forces over which they have little control. They are more concerned with fate, luck, or fortune, and a sense of destiny based almost on magic. This belief has little to do with the teachings of religion.

Belief in fate may be strong enough to alter a man's entire life and determine his goals and ambitions. He is sure that if the cards are "right," or the dice "hot," or the lucky number turns up, then things are "going his way." On the other hand, if luck is against him and the dice are "cold," he might as well not bother trying, because nothing good will come his way! If a man is lucky and things start rolling his way, anything is possible. But if a man is unlucky, then he is doomed to a miserable life filled with only empty dreams and disappointments.

Gambling is naturally associated with the idea of fate. But gambling also satisfies slum concern with excitement, smartness, and toughness. For example, just winning or losing provides excitement, but playing cards or pool requires toughness, or physical skill; betting on horse races requires smartness, or ability to outwit the odds-makers; and playing the numbers requires good luck. Obviously, there are many activities besides gambling which may satisfy the whole range of slum values.

AUTONOMY

Many slum men and women make a great display of their dislike of authority or any restrictions on their freedom. Often heard are the phrases: "Nobody's gonna push me around!" or, "I don't need nobody to care for me. I can take care of myself!" Strangely enough, however, the speaker of these bold words often seems to drive himself into situations that will restrict his freedom. Fate pushes him into excitement which results in trouble, causing a loss of his autonomy, that is, of control over his own activities. But actually, by indulging in these patterns of behavior, the law-breaking individual may be deliberately inviting his parents, or his wife, or the school authorities, or his boss, or the police to stop him. He may not admit it to himself but after some trouble-producing episode—a brawl or a drunken binge—he may definitely seek out a confining job or even a prison sentence. It is as if there were some comfort in the restriction, for restriction at least shows that someone is caring about him. But then, after a certain period of enduring this wished-for control by an outside source, he grows resentful and restless. He "breaks out" and involves himself in even more trouble and that starts the cycle over again! It is almost as if he were saying: "Save me from myself!"

THE STREET–CORNER GANG

The teen-age street-corner gang is a major adolescent group in slum society. Naturally, the chief concerns and values of youthful gang members are much the same as those of adults of their world. However, the corner gang has two additional values: belonging and status. In the adolescent, these values are best expressed when his behavior conforms to the adult concepts of toughness, smartness, autonomy, and so on, which have just been described.

BELONGING

The street-corner gang is a central force in the life of slum boys between the ages of 12 and 18. In many cases, the gang is the most stable and solid group they have ever known. Their ties to the gang are usually much stronger than those to their own families. And for many of the boys who have been raised in the woman-dominated households that are their typical experience of family life, the gang provides the first real opportunity to learn the essential roles of a man.

Because a gang offers these and other advantages (protection, security, companionship), it is vitally important to be a member who is in good standing. One becomes and remains a member of the gang by accepting and upholding its standards. And should those standards happen to violate middle-class laws and morals, the gang member will frequently respect the gang's values first. If he did not, he would be thrown out.

STATUS

Just like all adolescents, the members of the street-corner gang worry over their own status in their group and the status of the group itself. One way an individual can move up in status in the gang is by proving his toughness through athletic skill, strength, or bravery, or by proving his smartness by his ability to "razz" or "put on" his buddies. (The term "ranking" or "signifying" is sometimes used by youths to describe the jesting insults between members of a gang; the names show plainly that they realize that skill in word-play can help one to move up or down in the ranks of the gang.) Another way of achieving status is to do the things that adults can do: smoke, drink, gamble, stay out all night, and come and go as one pleases.

The standing of the gang itself among other gangs is called its "rep," that is, reputation, and reputation is based on a gang's toughness in comparison with other gangs. Many members feel their safety and security depend on their gang's rep, and gang wars often begin because members claim "we can't chicken out on a fight—our rep would be shot!" To "chicken out" would drag the gang down to the bottom of the status ladder and invite other gangs to make attacks upon it.

On the other hand, a gang's reputation may be based on peaceful and almost constructive standards. The rep of a street-corner gang often depends on who sets the values for a neighborhood: the local professional criminals or individuals in institutions such as the welfare department or the churches.

No matter what the rep of a gang, good or bad, the members want most of all to be considered "in." And what they do to achieve status and maintain membership is often considered less in terms of right or wrong, legal or illegal, moral or immoral than in terms of gang approval or disapproval.

DELINQUENT ACTS AS APPROVED BEHAVIOR

Almost every street-corner gang engages in some activities that violate established laws and ordinances. The most common violations are auto thefts, assaults, gang fights, petty pilfering, shoplifting, mugging, and purse snatching. Naturally, the gang members know that these acts are against the law: the boys are not stupid or mentally defective. Indeed, being a gang member demands a certain intelligence, and most gangs try to recruit the most "able" boys of the neighborhood.

Why then is crime a customary feature of gang life? Dr. Miller and his associates conclude that it is probably because lawbreaking activities are among the easiest and quickest means to achieve the values and standards of their world.

For example, the influence of slum culture patterns can be clearly seen in the typical gang war, once very common in many cities, and still very common in some cities. This is illustrated in the following description of a war between two gangs—the Diamonds and the Cobras.

A member or members of the Diamonds "trespass" on the claimed territory of the Cobras. While in the territory, the Diamonds commit an act which the Cobras consider a violation of their laws, an affront to their honor, and a clear challenge to their rep. Perhaps the Diamonds insulted a girl associated with the Cobras; but just the mere act of trespassing is seen as a deliberate provocation. In any case, the Cobras attack the trespassing Diamonds.

Later, the assaulted Diamonds return to their home territory and tell fellow gang members about the incident, usually stressing the unreasonableness of the attack ("I just looked at her! Hardly even said a word!") and the unfair advantage taken by the enemy ("About twenty of them jumped just the two of us!"). The highly exaggerated account excites the Diamonds. They must strike back to protect their honor and preserve their rep. War councils are held, allies are recruited, strategy is planned, messengers are dispatched, and pep talks are given to bolster the gang's strength and keep up the fighting spirit.

Sometimes the raid of the war party into enemy territory results in a full-scale fight. More often the enemy is nowhere to be seen or the police have been tipped off by an anonymous caller. When this happens, the gang members may express disgust and disappointment, but secretly they are relieved. Their honor has been avenged without injury. And the anonymous tipster probably belongs to one of the two rival gangs.

The pattern of the gang war between Diamonds and Cobras clarifies the motives behind some forms of delinquent behavior among slum youths. All the actions undertaken by the two gangs were conscious and positive steps to maintain their own status, and subconscious attempts to maintain the standards honored and respected in their own special culture.

But unfortunately, by their very nature, many standards of this slum culture almost automatically violate certain moral and legal standards of the middle class. This does not mean that the

Diamonds, the Cobras, or even Cool Bill Martin by their law-breaking acts are deliberately rebelling against values they do not share. Instead, Cool Bill and the gangs are primarily conforming to traditions that they *do* know and understand—as do their families and the neighborhood. Seen in this light, their acts cannot be considered completely hostile or directly in conflict with all of society, but rather as responses very much in harmony with their own culture.

Given this situation, can there be any hope for eliminating what middle-class people call delinquency among slum youths? Perhaps not immediately. They cannot be shown the error of their ways, for many of their ways seem right to their friends and families. Nor can the youths be taught to conform to other values overnight, for their own values have deep meaning for them.

Many feel that a long-term task in the future is to change the entire fabric of slum life so that lawful responses of youth will begin to be rewarding to them. Today, as during past years, many agencies and organizations, both government and private, are attempting to change the traditions of the slum and to re-align its major life patterns. Their ultimate goal, of course, is to replace trouble with achievement, toughness with pride, excitement with productivity, smartness with intellectual development, autonomy with self-confidence and self-control, and fate with ambition and opportunity.

Delinquency and
Social Status*

Does where a person lives and goes to school have more influence in determining his behavior than the social status of his family?

Does the social class composition of the school environment have more influence in determining the behavior of boys than the social class status of the family?

Is the class culture in which one is reared the main determinant producing delinquency?

Does middle-class status keep one from being a delinquent?

Is delinquency an essential feature of lower-class culture?

What is the background and life history of a juvenile delinquent? What is the "social status" of such a boy?

Consider two boys. Cliff Jones lives with his parents, brother, and sister in one side of a small frame house in a run-down section of town. The furniture is old and worn out and there are no rugs on the floors. There are no books anywhere in the house. Mr. Jones, who dropped out of school in the eighth grade, works as a helper with a roofing company—when there is work. Mrs. Jones has a bad heart, but is able to make a little money on Saturdays, working at the corner store.

Josiah H. Park's father runs a thriving insurance agency and the Parks live in an expensive suburb in a large brick house set on a big plot of well-kept lawn at some distance from the nearest neighbors. Inside there is wall-to-wall carpeting and, among the many rooms, a study with walls lined with well-filled bookcases

---

* Adapted from "The Distribution of Juvenile Delinquency in the Social Class Structure" by Albert J. Reiss, Jr., and Albert Lewis Rhodes, *American Sociological Review* (Washington, D.C.: American Sociological Association), Vol. 26, No. 5 (October 1961), pp. 720–732. Reprinted by permission.

extending to the ceiling. Both of Josiah's parents graduated from college. His mother cares for the house and garden and, for recreation, belongs to a dancing class composed of suburban housewives.

Which of these two boys is more likely to become a delinquent? ⌐

Certainly, most people would pick Cliff—it seems like common sense. Most sociologists, too, would probably nominate Cliff. But things are not so simple. Some scholars are convinced that high rates of delinquency may be found also in middle- and upper-status areas, but that the police and courts more often label boys of lower status as delinquents.*

HYPOTHESES ABOUT STATUS AND DELINQUENCY

There are two reasons why sociologists argue that more delinquency is recorded from among those of lower status. The first is that in the parts of town where they live there is a tradition of delinquency, so that a boy like Cliff will be likely to associate with other boys whose actions run afoul of the law. These are the slums—very different from the tree-lined lanes of Josiah's suburb.

The second argument is that if a boy like Cliff goes to a school with boys of middle status, he will be handicapped in competition with his classmates, will fall behind, and will end by resenting his difficult position and react by joining a gang. This, they say, allows him to ease his frustration by acquiring status as a member of the gang and "taking it out" on the community by violating its laws.

Two sociologists, Albert J. Reis, Jr., and Albert Lewis Rhodes, were not satisfied with these suppositions and determined to put them to the test.

PROCEDURES

The two sociologists became a research team, gathering information from over 9,000 white boys in Davidson County, Ten-

* See "Who Is a Delinquent and Who Is Not?" and "Middle-Class Delinquency" in this book.

nessee, which contains the city of Nashville. The boys were all attending one of the public, private, or parochial schools of the county.

Other information which they gathered about each boy included the occupation of his father, the composition and prestige of his school, and the delinquency rate of the districts he lived in. The delinquency rate is the figure reached by dividing the area's total of boys of juvenile court age by the number of them who are delinquent.

Then they separated the boys into three status groups according to the occupation of their fathers, as follows:

Low Status: All laborers, semiskilled operatives, and service workers (cooks, waiters, barbers, deliverymen, etc.). In this category the sociologists would have put Cliff Jones.

Middle Status: All craftsmen and artisans (electricians, mechanics, etc.), foremen, clerical workers in offices, managers and proprietors of small businesses, sales workers in wholesale and retail stores, technicians allied to the professional service, and protective service workers (policemen, firemen, etc.).

High Status: All managers, officials, and proprietors, and professional and semi-professional workers not included in the middle category, and sales workers in finance, insurance, and real estate. Josiah Park belongs in this class.

Next, the two sociologists classified each school according to the occupations of the fathers of the pupils in it. By this method they ended up with seven different types of school. One of the seven types of school was populated by the upper and middle status, taken together, and one by those whose fathers' occupations were low in status. But the remaining five types of schools had students whose fathers came from mixtures of the three levels of status, combined in varying proportions. For the sake of clarity only three of the types are discussed here: they offer a sample of the findings yielded by all the schools, for the conclusions they suggest are borne out by all the other schools.

FINDINGS

Boys like Josiah Park, from families of high status, who are in the two "lower" types of school, have somewhat lower rates of delinquency (3 and 8) than boys of lower status. But these rates of 3 and 8 are not lower than the rate of boys of low status who are in the school with the highest prestige (upper and upper-middle), for there the rate is 0 (Table 1).

TABLE 1
Rate of Delinquency per 100 White School Boys, and Occupational Status of Father and Status Structure of the School *

STATUS OF THE SCHOOL	OCCUPATIONAL STATUS OF FATHER		
	HIGH	MIDDLE	LOW
Upper and Upper Middle	4	3	0
Mixed, represents all status groups	3	6	9
Lower	8	15	16

* The figures in this table are the *rate* of delinquency. The *rate* tells how many boys, out of 100 in his classification, have ever been classified as delinquent by the court. Traffic offenses are not included in this table; since the research team discovered that including them would not alter the findings.

The right-hand column, telling about the boys, like Cliff Jones, from low-status families shows that when they are in the school that is low in prestige they have the highest of rates (16) which seems like common sense. But when they attend schools with a mixed status composition, their delinquency rate falls to 9 and to 0 in the upper and the upper-middle school. However, the research team is quick to point out that there were less than 100 boys of lower status in the high prestige school, and this is a small number from which to draw final conclusions.

One thing is certain: boys from families of high status have rates of delinquency which vary according to the type of school they attend. Equally important is the finding that boys whose families are low in status cannot be considered "naturally" delinquent. Those who attend schools of higher status have delinquency rates which are not higher than the rates of boys whose parents have had greater advantages.

It is clear, of course, that delinquency rates become higher as one goes from schools high in prestige to those which are lower. Thus the rates for boys of high status rise from 4 to 8, for those of middle status from 3 to 15, and, on reaching the sons of fathers whose occupations are low in status, from 0 to 16.

Finally, it already seems clear that boys from *families* of high status are less likely to become delinquents than boys from low, and similarly, boys from high status *schools* are less likely to be delinquents than those from low.

The sociologists then looked at an even larger picture—the delinquency rate of a whole residential area of the county. They separated the residential areas in the county into 10 categories, according to the delinquency rate in each. For example, a few sections (perhaps like Josiah's suburb) had a rate of less than 2 (2 delinquents per 100 boys), while others went as high as 17 or 18 (Table 2). Table 2 shows the relationship, in two of the seven kinds of school, between all three of these types of social status (family, school, area) and the delinquency of the boys. The two selected types of school are representative of all the other five.

Reading the top line across the page for the first type of mixed school population gives the figures for boys of high family status. From left to right, the *areas* they live in have increasingly high delinquency rates. The boys themselves show increasing rates of delinquency: 0, 2, 3, 10, 13, and 11. This shows that boys from the same kinds of homes and schools are drawn more into delinquency if they live in a high delinquency area.

On the second line the same facts are reported, this time for boys from middle family status. The same thing happens—the type of district influences how frequently a boy becomes delinquent. And the same holds true for lower-status boys (third line), going from 2 to 12, by type of district. (There is a drop to 9 in the highest delinquency area; but the sociologists explain that if they had had information about an area with an even higher rate, the rates for these boys would go up, perhaps to about 15.)

Now in the schools where the occupations of lower status are well represented, the figures from left to right give the record of the boys' delinquency according to each type of family status. Much the same increases appear. The most disadvantaged boys (last line) maintain low rates (2, 3, 3) in districts which

TABLE 2
Rate of Delinquency per 100 White School Boys, by Delinquency Rate of Residential Area, Status of School, and Occupational Status of Father

STATUS OF SCHOOL AND OCCUPATIONAL STATUS OF FATHER	DELINQUENCY RATE OF RESIDENTIAL AREA								
	0.0 to 1.9	2.0 to 3.9	4.0 to 5.9	6.0 to 7.9	8.0 to 9.9	10.0 to 11.9	12.0 to 13.9	14.0 to 15.9	16.0 to 17.9
Mixed (with managers and officials largely represented)									
High	0	2	3	. .	10	13	11	. .	. .
Middle	0	2	4	. .	6	9	13	. .	. .
Low	0	2	5	. .	8	12	9	. .	. .
Mixed (with laborers and machine operators represented)									
High	0	3	0	. .	4	9	. .	. .	11
Middle	2	5	6	. .	7	11	. .	. .	17
Low	2	3	3	. .	11	11	. .	. .	16

are not high in delinquency, but when they live in high-rate slum areas, the very same kind of boys show more delinquency (11, 11, and as high as 16). Such areas are found to have an established tradition of delinquency, so that young boys are more easily led into nonconforming behavior.*

With these findings, the sociologists were also able now to disprove the "status frustration" hypothesis—that boys of low status will feel rejected in schools attended by boys of higher status and join a delinquent gang to solve their problems. That this is

* See "The Slum: Opportunities for Crime and Delinquency" in this book.

not true can be seen here in both of the tables. Actually, these data reveal that the more the lower-class boy is in a minority in the school and residential community, the less likely he is to become a delinquent. For example, Table 1 tells that boys of low family status are *less* likely to become delinquent when they attend schools higher in status (rates of 0 and 9—as contrasted with a rate of 16 when they go to the school with low prestige).

TOWARD THE FUTURE

Most boys who are officially classed as delinquent in their teens do not become adult criminals. But which kinds of boys are the most likely to continue in crime? For clues, Reiss and Rhodes interviewed a small sample of 158 boys. They asked them to tell about their lives, with emphasis on two things: how they themselves saw their futures, and with whom they associated.

The two sociologists learned from their interviews that only a few of the boys (just over 1 percent) saw themselves as "career delinquents" and at the same time maintained close association with other offenders and even with some adult criminals as well. They were the most severe "problem boys."

The most numerous category of all was the "conformers"— boys who were guilty of only minor offenses or of none at all, who engaged in the usual kinds of play around school, and who spent time with their friends on occasional evenings. But this large group can be split in two. The larger portion of them were not only conformers but "achievers" as well. They had fairly high ambitions—to attend college, to enter business or the professions, to become active in civic affairs. The rest of the conformers lacked this drive. Rather, many of them appeared to be "killing time," with little thought for the future and their place in it.*

SUMMARY

The chief conclusion reached by Reiss and Rhodes is that among the 9,000 white boys they studied, there is no simple relationship between social status and delinquency.

* See "The Candidate for Delinquency" in this book.

More delinquents come from lower-status families, but a considerable number also have been raised in more advantaged homes. Further, boys, whatever their status, become delinquent more often when they attend schools of lower prestige and when they live in districts with high rates of delinquency.

The sociologists were able to reject the hypothesis that when boys of low status attend schools of greater prestige, they feel frustrated by the stiffer competition and join delinquent gangs to "get even." Finally, they found that few boys appear to be setting out upon lives of crime. In other words, many boys have no lasting commitment to delinquency. Despite an unpromising start, most of them develop into responsible citizens.

Middle-Class Delinquency*

What changes in the American economy, the educational system and the family system have given rise to a youth-dominated culture?

What features of the youth culture come out of the interaction of the youths themselves?

How does the youth culture generate delinquent behavior?

How does it happen that harmless activities and delinquent behavior may both be encouraged by the youth culture?

The greater part of the sociological research on delinquency in the United States has been based in the slums. The reasons are obvious. There is so much more delinquency to be found among disadvantaged slum youth—trapped by poverty, poor education, lack of opportunity, and other handicaps—that for a long time no one seemed to notice the delinquency of the middle class.

The middle class is very large. Most Americans, if asked to place themselves, claim to belong in it. Some sociologists think of American society as consisting of four classes: a lower class of unskilled manual workers; a working class of manual workers in semiskilled and skilled occupations (the "blue-collar" jobs); a middle class of "white-collar" workers and professionals; and an upper class which is the elite, distinguished from the middle class not so much by occupation as by wealth and prestige. Other sociologists divide Americans into three classes. They put **all** manual workers into one lower class. In either scheme, whether four classes or three, the middle class is the great core, growing larger, year by year, by additions from the class below. The suburban family is only one element in the middle class.

Professors Scott and Vaz, whose findings are presented in this selection, mention alcohol as playing a part in the youth culture. But they say nothing of drugs. Since 1968, the use of drugs has become too common

* Adapted from "A Perspective on Middle-Class Delinquency" by Joseph W. Scott and Edmund W. Vaz, *Canadian Journal of Economics and Political Science*, Vol. 29 (August 1963), pp. 324–335. Reprinted by permission.

in high schools to be overlooked. In some schools smoking "pot" has become almost a ceremonial. No one has yet discovered whether there is less drinking now among young people, but there is no doubt at all about the increasing use of drugs. A great difference between the two indulgences, however, is that parents may introduce adolescents to drink. Peers introduce them to drugs.

As Ted and Louise and Rich and Nancy packed up their belongings after a long, hot day at the beach, they really had nothing in mind except to drive home to the suburbs and maybe stop by at a roadside snack bar for hamburgers and fried clams. It had been a good day all in all, though Ted was a little miffed because Rich had shown him up at swimming and handball and had then started treating him like a kid brother rather than the 17-year-old he was.

When they got to the place where the car was parked, Rich could not find his keys at first, and this gave Ted a chance to admire the red convertible with its black-cushioned upholstery parked directly behind them. "This is the kind I'm going to get next year," he claimed, circling the sports model, "not some broken-down job like Rich has." With that, he opened the door, climbed into the driver's seat, motioned Louise to follow him, and shouted back to Rich and Nancy, "Forget the keys, crawl in, and we'll give this little number a ten-minute test run." Nancy hesitated, murmuring something about the time and about not wanting to use property that didn't belong to her; but Rich, not to be outdone by the competition, quickly jumped in, dragging her, too.

Together, the two boys experimented with the ignition, using a trick they had once seen demonstrated to get a motor started without benefit of a key. Two minutes later they were moving down the sandy road towards the highway, now laughing and joking, transistor blaring and engine throbbing. "Okay," announced Rich from the rear, "now let's make like the Bonneville salt flats." Rising to the challenge, Ted soon had the speedometer up to 95. He felt great, being the one in the driver's seat.

Twenty-five minutes of joy riding later, the "Bonneville Four," to the surprise and horror of both themselves and their ultra-respectable parents, were in the hands of the police, charged with car theft. How had it all happened? How was it possible that *they* had become juvenile delinquents?

Most of us are accustomed to thinking of juvenile delinquency as a product of poverty, as a pattern of behavior most frequently found among the lower classes of society. Yet in recent years there has been increasing evidence that middle-class youths, like Ted and Rich, Louise and Nancy, are also likely to be offenders against the law. Since their law-breaking is obviously not the result of economic need, how can it be explained? In the face of this puzzling development, two sociologists—Joseph W. Scott and Edmund W. Vaz—have attempted not only to describe the dominant forms of delinquent behavior among middle-class youth but to analyze its existence in terms of the structural, or basic, changes that have taken place in North American society over the past three-quarters of a century. The foundation on which the two sociologists built their theory is research on the social world of adolescents which was undertaken in recent years by leading sociologists.

What are some of the changes that have occurred during this period that might account for the growth of middle-class juvenile delinquency? First and foremost is the development of a distinctive middle-class youth culture, by which sociologists mean the specific pattern of activities engaged in by middle-class teenagers and the standards of conduct and values which they follow. The existence of a separate teen-age culture, one which functions either apart from or in conflict with the dominant adult culture, has been taken for granted for so long by Americans that it is hard to realize that it is actually a relatively recent social phenomenon.

Middle-class young people were not always characterized by rebelliousness against the adult world, by clannishness among members of their own age group, or by a special set of interests, values, and type of behavior. Indeed, young people 75 years ago probably had more in common with their parents, in attitude and outlook on life, than they would with today's teen-agers. One reason for this is that adolescence then constituted a much shorter period. It started later and ended earlier. Comparatively few middle-class youths went to college. Therefore, jobs, and with them adult financial responsibilities, were undertaken at a much earlier age, leaving the individual free to pursue exclusively adolescent activities for only a brief time. And even then, the realities of life usually forced young people to concentrate more on preparing themselves for the future than on having a good time.

But even more influential than the pressure of economic necessity was the pressure of "the Protestant ethic" upon middle-class Americans and those striving to enter middle-class society. By "Protestant ethic" sociologists refer to the belief that such virtues as industry, thrift, self-discipline, and individual integrity will be rewarded by economic success in life. It is a belief historically connected with certain forms of Protestantism. And America at the turn of the century seemed to offer dramatic proof of the truth of this conviction. For, as the country emerged from the frontier period, the land and economy offered unparalleled opportunities for the accumulation of wealth, for upward mobility, or the bettering of one's social status, and for employment based on the possession of technical skills. Hard work and good character truly *were* in most instances rewarded, and the middle classes were thereby strengthened in their belief and encouraged to pass it on to their children.

To instill the energy, determination, and moral strength necessary to meet the challenges of an expanding economy, considerable emphasis was given in the home to the formal character training of children. At the same time, fathers, by their devotion to work, preoccupation with production, and reliance on self-help, pointed up definite goals for their children and provided clear-cut examples of the way in which "getting ahead" could be accomplished. Schooling, too, was a serious business; children were taught that what mattered was what they could accomplish, not how pleasing their personalities were or how cooperative their attitudes. Teachers held undisputed authority, discipline was harsh, and scholarship rigorous.

Neither home life nor school life allowed young people sufficient time to develop extensive relationships with their peers, or others of their own age and background. A youth's role as student, together with the duties imposed on him at home and the parentally encouraged habits of "saving for college" and "working after school," served to keep him occupied, indoors, and off the streets. His companions were most likely to be his own brothers and sisters. Associations with his peers were time-consuming and often costly, and middle-class youth were not inclined to waste either time or money.

After World War I, however, the economy, and with it the structure of the American family, underwent dramatic change. Coupled with the growth of technology and the declining demand for unskilled and semiskilled labor was a decline in the number of proprietors and the massive centralization of industry. This structural upheaval severely restricted the upward mobility of the lower-placed worker. Furthermore, the leveling of income and social resources favored the mass production of educated and specialized personnel for the labor market. As the number of college-trained people increased, industry could afford to become highly selective in its choice of personnel. This meant that the criteria for recruitment and promotion changed and that qualities other than technical competence became crucial. With so many able people to choose from, employers began to place greater emphasis on the quality of "well-roundedness" in their employees. Thus, conformity to the norms of the Protestant ethic became impracticable and were discarded in favor of the social skills and values of a new morality—the social ethic, in which the greatest value is placed upon "getting on well with people."

Under these different social and economic conditions there took place a gradual transformation in the makeup of the family, in family patterns, and in child-rearing practices. The traditional, patriarchally controlled family gave way to the more democratic unit in which parents and children shared in decision-making. Standards guiding parent-child relationships became blurred, and the family atmosphere became increasingly permissive. In contrast to the acquisition of technical skills and ethical values for the achievement of goals, the means for getting ahead and for gaining prestige became in these new circumstances difficult to understand and even more difficult to teach. The displacement of old values in the spheres of work and social relations made it almost impossible for parents to know how to instruct their offspring in the adolescent role.

The family was not the only institution to feel the effects of corporate industry's changing needs. The school, too, was transformed, but, unlike the family, whose role contracted as the century wore on, the school's role expanded. Before long it was exercising the primary responsibility in society for "socializing" the child, that is, for preparing him to get along successfully with his fellow students during the educational process and with his employers and colleagues during his career—in other words, for seeing to it that he was "adjusted" to the culture in which he lived. To help develop these well-rounded individuals wanted by the business world, the schools focused more and more on developing in their charges certain personality characteristics thought to be desirable for success in life.

Under such conditions the school becomes noticeably more easygoing and permissive, fixed standards of performance tend to be abandoned on the ground that they restrain the child, and the whole learning experience is slowly but surely transformed into a painless process. With drastically relaxed academic requirements, school work for the teen ager becomes routine, and since household chores are few and light in the more relaxed family atmosphere, the middle-class adolescent has little work to absorb his time throughout the day or evening. With increased leisure time, peers become available and the emergence of peer groups possible.* The teen-ager who has witnessed how important social standing is to his parents and the emphasis they place on "keeping up with the Joneses" also begins to court the good opinion of his peers. Furthermore, both his parents and teachers encourage group-belonging as a means of winning social prestige and recognition.

Since most adolescents have only a hazy idea of what society expects of them and of what constitutes "right conduct," they are particularly open to the influence of the peer group, which is easier to follow than the uncertain example set by adults. In the group the individual no longer has to decide for himself what is "valuable" or "good" or "correct." He merely has to conform to whatever behavior patterns prevail. And since there are no other

* See "Age-Mates: The World of the French Child," in *Life in Families* in this *Readings in Sociology* Series.

standards to guide him, there is little justification for not conforming to the peer group. The high school, too, by setting adolescents apart from the rest of society for their academic training and by virtually compelling them to carry out the major part of their lives with others who are their own age, contributes to the growth of peer groups and to the maintenance of a separate youth culture.

Ted, Louise, Rich, and Nancy were responding to the values of the youth culture.

What does membership in a peer group do for an adolescent like Ted? First of all, it gives him a sense of security through the knowledge that he is valued and accepted by others. This social approval gives notice to peers and parents alike that the teen-ager is socially adjusted, and this in turn can lead to further rewards at home because parents want their children to be successful and will judge that success largely according to how well their children are esteemed by their friends. In this way the older generation helps reinforce the values of the adolescent culture.

Second, peer-group membership gives the teen-ager his first taste of independence, for it is within the group that he tries out new ideas, shares secret emotions, and develops a set of values that may run counter to what parents and teachers have previously held up to him. Here, for instance, he can probe into the mysteries of sex without the nagging intervention of adults. Here, too, he can rebel against academic requirements and standards and unite with others in waging guerrilla warfare against what he perceives to be the tyranny of the system, with its emphasis on grades and production. Success or failure in the schoolroom is obviously less important to the teen-ager than acceptance by the peer group, which in turn requires a rigid conformity to its group standards.

The compulsion to conform would seem to be a small price to pay for what membership in the peer group confers. Through the group the adolescent is offered access to parties, dances, dates, popular girls (or boys), the latest style, big events, and other "social" advantages. Conversely, the student who abides by other standards out of concern for studies, good grades, or a sense of individuality is not so likely to be sought after by the opposite sex. In the present-day high school it is the active student, the boy or girl who engages in social affairs, extracurricular activities, and athletics, who ranks highest in the adolescent culture and, often, with the teachers as well.

Sociologists Scott and Vaz identify "partying," "joy riding," "drag racing," drinking, gambling, and various types of sex behavior as among the dominant forms of adolescent conduct within the middle-class youth culture. Such activities usually involve both boys and girls and offer adolescents an opportunity to gain status and social success among their peers.

Having already pinpointed conformity as the keynote in the youth culture, Scott and Vaz argue that the bulk of middle-class delinquency occurs in the course of customary nondelinquent activities and that it falls within the limits of adolescent group norms. In other words, it starts out as legitimate activities such as dating, parties, dances, or the possession of an automobile. Thus, they feel, in order to account for middle-class delinquency it is not necessary to look for a separate "delinquent subculture."

What is the mechanism which pushes lawful activities over the fine line dividing them from unlawful activities? Scott and Vaz find this in the tendency of some individual members of the peer group to initiate or explore behavior which will impress their friends and which will therefore be socially rewarded. In the course of everyday activities and relationships of the youth culture, veiled competition for status leads to varying attempts to "be different" or to "start something." These exploratory acts are likely to be tentative and uncertain at first, but because others are involved in the new type of behavior and help to make it something more than it was at first, such small scarcely noticeable acts gradually lead to unexpected behavior that goes beyond the limits of what is permitted. But each succeeding exploratory act is so small an addition to the previously accepted pattern that it is quite possible that those involved may never at any stage in the process perceive the behavior as delinquent. Ted did not plan to steal a car, or even to joy ride at first. But he was excited and driven on by the desire to impress Rich and the girls, who, like all of their "crowd," greatly admired fast cars and envied fast drivers.

How, precisely, does delinquent behavior arise from respectable behavior during the course of socially acceptable activities? The party provides a good example. Proper party behavior is first learned by the child at home through watching his parents and other adults on such occasions. As he reaches adolescence, not only do his parents expect him to participate in social activities, but they often give tacit consent to his "having a taste" or to his "spiking" the party punch. Some parents, in fact, encourage teen-age drinking in the home as a means of teaching young people "how to handle liquor." In this way drinking becomes acceptable. But as the drinking pattern develops among adolescents it generates its own morality, its special game rules, and its particular rewards. Among older adolescents, informal drinking bouts to test one's capacity for alcoholic beverages are not uncommon. Indeed the approval given the adolescent who can "hold his liquor" follows adult lines. On the other hand, adolescent intoxication is not generally condemned since it simply represents an unsuccessful attempt to conform to the rules of the game.

Likewise, the possession of a car, harmless in itself, may lead to delinquency. An automobile has become an integral feature of middle-class youth culture, for without it, young people must be chauffeured to movies, sports events, and, especially galling to boys, to dates. Having a car, on the other hand, builds up the teen-ager's self-image and gives him a large, measure of social status among his peers. By the way in which he presents it and handles it he can add to that prestige, and in this way he may often come into competition with others. This struggle for status may start with simply "dressing" the automobile, but can easily lead to sporting "duals or Hollywood mufflers," "joy riding," "drag racing," and ultimately to "playing chicken" at a hundred miles an hour. It was the competition between Ted and Rich, together with their knowledgeability about cars, which led them into a delinquent action which otherwise they would never have undertaken.

Delinquent sex behavior among middle-class adolescents also emerges from culturally approved activity, and can be explained as a variation on the encouraged patterns of dating. Parents, concerned that their children be attractive to the opposite sex and engaged in "healthy," "normal" activities, give their blessing to restricted forms of physical contact between teen-age boys and girls such as holding hands, dancing, good-night kisses, and, under certain conditions such as "going steady," to the initial stages of "necking"—justifying such contacts as indications of "social maturity" and part of "growing up." But, just as in other areas, innovative and exploratory behavior emerges from the dating relationship and may rapidly go beyond the limits of responsible conduct.

While both sexes engage in the dominant behavior patterns and activities in the youth culture, there are some recurrent situations in which only boys participate. Yet the veiled quest for social recognition is as important in an all-male group as in the overall teen-age culture. But here efforts at innovation are likely to take a less sophisticated form, one that is frequently related to the need to assert one's masculinity. For instance, groups of boys "hanging about" at night, returning from a football game, or simply wasting time "roughhousing," often engage in acts of destruction such as "stomping" on the hoods and roofs of automobiles, letting out air from tires, ripping antennae from automobiles, and breaking street lights. However, "muggings," "rolling drunks," breaking and entering, or armed robbery rarely occur among middle-class boys. Such behavior of a violent nature, usually undertaken to steal money, reflects values generally foreign to middle-class culture.

Under what circumstances is the middle-class teen-ager most likely to become involved in delinquent behavior? Scott and Vaz find that the actual performance of delinquent acts depends largely on the opportunity to carry them out and that this opportunity results from participation in legitimate activities. One condition for delinquent conduct is, of course, access to whatever is requisite for participating in the teen-age culture—such as cars, teen-age girls, alcoholic beverages, pocket money, the latest style, and so forth. Those without access to any of these "social objects" are extremely unlikely to become part of the middle-class teenage crowd and are therefore unlikely to participate in the legitimate social activities which so often lead other teen-agers into juvenile delinquency.

Another influence toward delinquent behavior is the particular aspect of the youth-culture activity which is impressed upon the individual adolescent. For instance, some teen-agers believe that "stirring up a little excitement" is crucial to participation, others that having a car is the only "right" way to be "in with the crowd," still others that sexual adventures or drinking a lot are necessary for success. To the degree that an adolescent favors all or various combinations of such activities as a means of taking part in the youth culture he is likely to become involved in delinquent behavior.

In addition, Scott and Vaz find that big cities with their abundance of movies, nightclubs, bars, bohemian coffee houses, discotheques, and jazz dens, insofar as they serve as organized opportunities for middle-class adolescents to engage in a wide variety of "sophisticated" and novel behavior with members of the opposite sex, are more conducive to delinquent behavior than the main street of a small town or the local 4-H Club in a rural area.

The two sociologists concluded that no special motives need be found to explain delinquent behavior in the middle class. At no time does the middle-class teen-ager turn from legitimate to illegitimate means to attain his ends. Ted did not engage in delinquent behavior because he had rejected more acceptable goals or because he had been frustrated in his attempts to be accepted by his age mates. The seeds of delinquency in the middle-class adolescent lay rather in his exposure to the culturally esteemed patterns themselves. Therefore, Scott and Vaz conclude, delinquent behavior can best be understood through knowledge of the legitimate youth culture and its connections to the community.

White-Collar Criminality*

What are the characteristics of white-collar crime and of white-collar criminals?

How are the white-collar criminals and their criminal behavior unlike the crimes and criminals of the slums?

Do the public and the courts take a different attitude to white-collar crime than to crime committed by the poor?

In April 1969, the newspapers reported that the United States Military Academy at West Point had been sold 25,000 pounds of uninspected meat. Two cousins, heads of a very large meat company, who had been awarded the contract to supply the cadet school were found using false certificates which declared that the meat they were delivering had passed inspection as of "high quality."

For six years the two cousins had made profits from their contract to supply meat to West Point—profits which would not have been so large if they had sold properly inspected meat. One of the men had been convicted, years earlier, of bribing an Army sergeant to accept substandard meat. In 1968, he and his relative were found guilty of offering for sale more than twelve thousand pounds of meat which the court described as "putrid." They were fined one dollar!

At last, however, the cousins' luck had run out. For their most recent offenses the fine was not one dollar; it was $8800! In the six years during which they cheated the Army, one may be sure their profits were far greater than the fine.

The point of importance in this true story of shady business is how easy it had been to cheat, year after year, and how mild was the punishment, when it came at last.

---

* Adapted from "White-Collar Criminality" by Edwin H. Sutherland, *American Sociological Review* (Washington, D.C.: American Sociological Association), Vol. 5, No. 1 (February 1940), pp. 1–12. Reprinted by permission.

The newspapers are full of stories like this one. There are stories of price-fixing by drug companies, of defective autos sold by car makers, of fraudulent "games" run by gasoline companies and supermarkets, of excessive rentals by greedy slumlords, and so on.

In many cases the wrongdoer is never punished. General Motors, for example, recalled thousands of defective cars and undid the damage. But nothing was said of the fact that the cars were represented at the time they were sold as being in perfect order.

The ghetto dweller can be evicted for not paying his rent, but the slumlord will receive only token warnings for overcharging his tenants or failing to supply heat as required by law. A slum youth may be thrown into jail for stealing trinkets from a Five-and-Ten, but drug manufacturers will get only a scolding for stealing millions of dollars by overcharging sick and elderly people.

In all these instances the established and respected business class in society is permitted to engage in behavior which, if the doer had been poor and unknown, would have brought on punishment by the courts. This was noted in 1940 by a sociologist whose description of it has become a classic. He called it "white-collar criminality."

SUTHERLAND ON CRIME

When Edwin H. Sutherland, a professor of sociology at Indiana University, wrote his study of "white-collar criminality," he was a revolutionary of sorts, for he questioned the common myth that nice, respectable people do not break the law. His work challenged the criminologists, police, lawyers, judges—indeed, everyone—who claimed crime was only the behavior of the poor. What Sutherland actually did was to overturn the existing theories of criminology based solely on statistical evidence. For example, the police and court records of his time (and today, also) showed that only 2 *percent* of the persons committed to prisons belonged to the white-collar class, meaning business and professional people. And often—but of course not always—they are influential and well-to-do. But the statistics referred to criminals handled by the police and criminal and juvenile courts for such crimes as murder, assault, burglary, robbery, larceny, and drunkenness. Looking at the figures, the criminologists of Sutherland's day noted that few business and professional people were arrested and that crime appeared to be concentrated among the poor, which meant chiefly the lower class. Therefore, said the criminologists, crime must be caused by poverty or the psychological and social conditions of the poor, such as feeblemindedness, insanity, poor environment, and poor family life.

Sutherland, however, reasoned that crime really had little to do with poverty and certainly was not restricted to poor people. Crime was widespread throughout all levels of society, and the criminologists, he declared, had been misled by faulty statistics which overlooked, for one thing, all the criminal behavior of business and professional people—that is, white-collar crime. What was needed was a conception of the offender that was not tinged at all with the idea of occupation or social class.

In defense of his theory, Sutherland offered a veritable catalog of business and professional crimes which never had appeared on court records or police blotters. And Sutherland might just as well have been describing the situation that exists today as the world of 1940. It may be that white-collar crime has not increased, but it is certainly true that we have become aware of it, and today more and more business and professional offenses are recognized as crime and treated accordingly.

ROBBER BARONS AND CORPORATE CROOKS

The tales about the "robber barons" of the 19th century are part of American folklore. The vast fortunes of today's "best families" often were created out of human suffering. For example, the most profitable cargo of the New England sea captains was slaves. Commodore Vanderbilt, when asked if his railroads should serve the public interest, is reported to have made the famous remark: "The public be damned!" And another railroad president, A. B. Stickney, once told sixteen of his cohorts: "I have the utmost respect for you gentlemen individually, but as railroad presidents I wouldn't trust you out of my sight with my watch." Today's white-collar criminals are not so bold. An increased awareness of public opinion, plus somewhat stricter federal regulations, have made any modern merchant princes who break the law less candid. Yet, examples of white-collar crime are still uncovered daily in the routine investigations of land speculation companies, railways, insurance firms, munitions makers, banks, public utilities, stock brokerages, and real estate offices. In fact, Sutherland's comment is still true: that a greater amount of important crime often can be found on the financial pages than on the front pages of newspapers. Almost any representative of any business can describe scores of crooked dealings in his own occupation. In fact, Sutherland gained much of the material for his study simply by asking doctors, lawyers, engineers, undertakers, retailers, and many others, "What crooked practices are there in your occupation?"

In business, white-collar crime usually takes the form of misrepresentation in financial statements or in advertising, bribery of public officials, embezzlement or misappropriation of funds, tax frauds, misleading packaging, or "kickbacks" for favors. Al Capone, the famous Mafia gangster of the 1920s, once called business the "legitimate racket," and it is no coincidence that many members of the crime syndicates have switched from risky dealings in drugs or gambling to the control of legal enterprises, such as the food, liquor, dry cleaning and vending machine trades.*

Crime is just as widespread in the professions, although professional societies tend to keep better control, or more complete silence, over the illegal practices of their members. The medical profession, for example, probably has less criminality than others, yet it cannot be denied that there are illegal sales of drugs to drug addicts, illegal operations, false testimony in accident cases, overcharging, charging for unnecessary treatment or operations, and fee-splitting.

The Extent of White-Collar Crime

Any accurate comparison of white-collar crimes with the crimes of the poor is probably impossible, simply because few records are kept of white-collar corruption. Sutherland, however, demonstrated the extent and enormity of white-collar crime by presenting a few illustrations, taken from the newspapers of

* See "Organized Crime and Its Social Effects" in this book.

the time. It is interesting that he listed the following offense among other examples: Of the cans of ether sold to the Army for medical purposes between 1923 and 1925, over 70 percent were rejected because of impurities. And it was in the 1960s that the Army was sold unsafe meat. This kind of cheating is made possible by systematic bribing of inspectors and purchasers who are supposed to be safeguarding the Army's interests. But we do not hear that any inspector or buyer has been called to account for his part in the wrong-doing. If Sutherland were writing today he might add to these instances of white-collar crime some other abuses of power and trust, such as: price-fixing by electronics companies; the granting of a contract to a space agency in return for favors to men who had influence with the government; and perhaps the best-known case, the admission by certain automobile manufacturers that they had been selling cars which supposedly had passed certain tests of safety, but which were actually dangerous to drive.

Of course, most businessmen are honest. On the other hand, however, these examples refer to some of the largest, best-known, and most respected corporations, not just the small-time quacks, ambulance chasers, deadbeats, con men, and fly-by-night swindlers. The difference is that the small-time offenders are often caught and punished; the white-collar offenders often are not.

THE COST OF WHITE-COLLAR CRIME

The true cost of white-collar crime is hard to assess, but it far exceeds any costs charged to what is commonly known as the criminal element in our society.

Sutherland offers as an example the story of a chain store executive who in one year embezzled $600,000, a sum six times the annual losses from 500 burglaries and robberies at all the stores in the chain. Today, we could count in the cost of graft uncovered in an urban renewal project and the theft by New York workers in a poverty program of thousands of dollars intended for the poor. This last offense was effected by writing false names on thousands of checks, cashing them, and pocketing the money.

The financial loss to the victims of white-collar crimes, great as it is, may be less important than its damage to social relations.

As Sutherland pointed out, white-collar crimes betray trust and therefore create distrust. The effect is to lower social morale and bring about social disorganization on a large scale. Sutherland's analysis proved frighteningly true in the sixties, when angry, frustrated blacks rioted in many cities, their targets being slum landlords who demanded excessive rents and supermarkets which charged higher prices for groceries in the ghettos than they charged in the suburbs.

Recognizing and Defining White-Collar Crime

White-collar crime is real crime, was Sutherland's theme. But he added that it is not usually called crime, and calling it crime will not make it worse—just as refusing to call it crime does not make it better. He spoke of it as crime only to bring it to the attention of criminologists.

Sutherland's point, of course, was that criminologists had ignored or overlooked white-collar crime largely because, as noted above, it did not turn up in official, statistical form. He went on to suggest that criminologists expand their investigation (and definition) of crime by adding to the records of court convictions four other measures of criminal behavior.

First, decisions by agencies *other* than the courts should be studied, too. Administrative boards, bureaus, and commissions often deal with white-collar practices which are in violation of the criminal laws. The Food and Drug Administration, for example, may stop drug companies from distributing potentially harmful products or from making expansive claims about a drug's curative powers. They stop the practice of adding to food cheap and sometimes harmful ingredients. The Federal Trade Commission stops dishonest advertising messages and forces manufacturers to call back defective products. And the Securities and Exchange Commission brings suit against stock brokers who give false tips to push up the price of certain stocks. And there should be added some of the practices which regulatory bodies examine. Bar associations and medical societies, for instance, pass judgment on the behavior of lawyers and doctors which could, in some cases, be called criminal, but which never reaches the law courts.

Second, any behavior—no matter by whom—which might have a reasonable chance of conviction in court, should be defined as criminal. Criminologists do not hesitate to use the case history of a person with a *known* background of crime, even though he may never have been convicted. They are also justified if they include in the statistics white-collar criminals who have never been convicted, if there is clear evidence of their wrongdoing. For example, Sutherland stated that at the time he was writing as many as 90 percent of all embezzlement cases were never brought to trial. This is because, since a conviction and jail sentence would prevent the embezzler from paying back the stolen funds to his employer, the employer sees it as against his own interest to report the matter. It goes undetected by the courts; but it is crime, just the same.

Third, criminal behavior should be defined as criminal, even if an actual conviction or arrest is prevented by pressure brought to bear on the court, the police, or the regulatory agency. For example, successful racketeers have become almost immune to the law because, by their threats, they frighten witnesses and public officials into silence; or they may buy their silence. However, criminologists still recognize that these men are "criminals."

Finally, Sutherland said that persons accessory to white-collar crimes, that is, accomplices, should be included in the statistics of crime, just as is done in the case of crimes of the poor. When the FBI investigates a kidnapping, it does not stop by arresting only the person who carried away the victim. It may catch and convict a score of other people who aided in the kidnapping by driving the getaway car, writing the ransom notes, or hiding the victim. In contrast, prosecution of white-collar criminals frequently stops with only one offender, as in the case of the man who sold unsafe meat, whose story was told above.

Graft usually involves deals between politicians and businessmen, but prosecutions are usually limited just to the public officials. "Boss" Pendergast of Kansas City, a notorious character of Sutherland's time, was finally convicted for failing to report as income the $315,000 in bribes he received from insurance companies, but the insurance companies were never brought to trial. Often, one or two officials of a company will be sacrificed: if a crooked deal is discovered they take the blame for the entire company or industry, though many other individuals must be involved.

Upper- and Lower-Class Crime: The Differences

When the statistical base for measuring and defining crime is broadened, the general description of criminality is about the same in both white-collar and other offenses. The only difference between the two types of crime is in the incidentals, not in the essentials.

The biggest difference is in how the law is enforced. For example, crimes of the lower class and the poor are usually handled by policemen, public prosecutors, probation officers, and judges, with punishment in the form of fines or imprisonment. On the other hand, crimes of the white-collar class may result in either no official action at all, or in suits for damages before civil justices. White-collar crimes are handled by inspectors, administrative boards, or commissions, and the punishment comes in the form of warnings, "cease and desist" orders, occasionally the loss of a license, or, in extreme cases, fines and prison sentences. Obviously, white-collar criminals are treated leniently and, as a result, they are not regarded as real criminals, either by themselves or the general public. The difference in treatment is due almost entirely to the position and power of the business or professional criminals.

Ironically, the white-collar criminal's social and business standing also puts him in a good position to determine the laws that will govern and regulate his own behavior. Congressmen, legislative bodies, and governmental agencies all respond directly to the power and pressure wielded by the big financial interests. A modern instance is the tobacco growers who have attempted to play down the warning on cigarette packs and to stop proposed regulation by Congress of the TV advertising of cigarettes.

In sharp contrast to the power of white-collar criminals is the weakness of their victims. Consumers, investors, and stockholders are, but for small exceptions here and there, unorganized, lacking in technical knowledge, and unable to muster the very great sums of money needed for legal battles. In short, white-collar crime flourishes best where powerful business and professional men come into contact with persons who are weak. On the other hand, many lower-class crimes are committed against persons of wealth and power. Considering the comparative strength of the two victims, it is no wonder that it is the lawbreakers who are poor who usually get caught. For them, crime really does *not* pay.

DEMOLISHING THE POVERTY THEORY

On three grounds Sutherland dismissed the theory that crime was concentrated in the slums and caused by poverty.

First, as already noted, the general theory was based on misleading statistics which completely ignored all white-collar crime. (This was in 1940.)

Second, the generalization that crime feeds on poverty or slum conditions did not apply to white-collar criminals. Most of them were not poor, nor feebleminded, nor deprived, nor discriminated against. Even if poverty had been so broadly defined that it could include periods of economic depression, no correlation could be made with business crimes. If anything, corporate crime seemed to rise in times of plenty rather than in periods of want.

Third, he claimed, a theory of poverty could not even explain the causes of lower-class crime itself. If the description of criminal behavior is really the same for all types of offenders, and if poverty cannot explain such behavior in the business and professional class, it cannot explain similar behavior in the lower class, either. According to Sutherland, poverty may explain why in the lower class people commit certain crimes (robbery and burglary) rather than others (embezzling and stock cheating), but it cannot explain the tendency to crime found at every level of society.

SUTHERLAND'S THEORY OF CRIME

After showing the shortcomings of the conventional theory of criminality, Sutherland developed his own explanation of crime, which is accepted by many of today's criminologists.

First, both white-collar and lower-class criminal behavior must be *learned,* just as any other type of behavior is learned. And it is learned by direct or indirect association with people who already practice it. Moreover, the newcomers to crime must become more and more isolated from individuals who practice or believe in law-abiding behavior. Whether a person becomes a criminal depends on the frequency and the intimacy of his contacts with one or the other of the two kinds of behavior, law-abiding or criminal.

Men who become white-collar criminals generally come from good homes and good neighborhoods, graduate from college, and, to some degree at least, most of them probably cherish some ideals of proper conduct. Then, with little selection or choice on their own part, they manage to get into business situations where criminal practices are accepted. Cut off from more law-abiding businessmen, the young executives also become part of a criminal way of life. For example, a practice the young man is likely to learn very early is that of "padding" his expense account (charging the costs of his private pleasure to the firm) and so actually robbing the firm or its shareholders.

Similarly, lower-class criminals start their careers in run-down slum neighborhoods, where they meet delinquents who teach them techniques of crime, criminal attitudes, and a contempt for the "squares" and the police.

Secondly, criminal behavior succeeds and persists because the community is not organized solidly against it. Individuals and groups may be so occupied with their own personal concerns that they pay little attention to the general welfare of the community. For example, scores of Better Business Bureaus and Crime Commissions are formed across the country by business and professional people to try to stop burglary, robbery, syndicated crime, or swindling, but they often overlook any breaking of the law by their own members.

Finally, society may enact laws to discourage criminal behavior, but all the while other social forces work to encourage it. In business, for instance, the "rules of the game" sometimes may conflict with the legal regulations and restrictions. And even the most honest businessman is sometimes forced to adopt the illegal methods used by his competitors if his business is to survive at all. He has to decide if it is worth the price of his honesty to play the game *their* way.

Sutherland's challenge to the old concepts and his exposé of "respectable crooks" did not have the effect of reducing white-collar lawbreaking. Like lower-class crime, there is still plenty of it. Even though certain practices have come to be called "crimes," many business and professional men continue to engage in them.

Of course, Sutherland being a student of society and not a reformer, did not intend to reform anything—other than the defi nition of crime. His study of white-collar crime made a powerful impression upon the sociologists of his day, and his definition of crime so as to include white-collar offenses is still accepted. His new theory of the causes of crime has changed the point of view of all sociological studies of criminal behavior since his time.

Teen-Agers Who Steal*

Since other sources are unreliable, could it be that youth would report truthfully on their own delinquency? Would a self-report scale of theft be reliable?

What are some of the variables which will produce important differences between the occasional thief and the one who steals often?

Would the self-report theft scale hold good for different communities, for example: suburban, rural farm, and nonfarm?

Will a youth's score on the theft scale be a reliable indication that he will continue in delinquent behavior?

Is the amount of stealing greater among adolescents with working mothers than among those whose mothers stay at home?

Sure, I swipe things. Who doesn't? Sometimes I take money from my old lady. She keeps it in a jar in her bureau. She gets a little angry, but it blows over. Other times I pick up a few things at the Five-and-Ten, if you know what I mean. A couple of times me and some other guys have even taken cars for rides. You know, we just rod around outside of town and then drop it off somewhere.

—Jerry Bruckner, 13.

"Jerry Bruckner" is an average student who comes from an average middle-class home that, on the surface at least, is no more troubled than any other. He is liked by most of his classmates and is thought by many to be a leader. Some other classmates, however, feel he is a bully and a braggart.

Jerry is also a thief. He steals from his mother's household funds, from the lockers of his classmates, and from Woolworth's.

* Adapted from "Social Correlates of Early Adolescent Theft" by Robert A. Dentler and Lawrence J. Monroe, *American Sociological Review* (Washington, D.C.: American Sociological Association), Vol. 26, No. 5 (October 1961), pp. 733–743. Reprinted by permission.

In the eyes of the law, Jerry would be considered a delinquent. However, Jerry has never been caught.

Jerry is one of the small percentage of teen-agers who commit illegal acts.* The questions that teachers, parents, and sociologists ask about Jerry are obvious: "What makes him a delinquent?" and "How does he differ from other teen-agers?"

Unfortunately, the first question may never be answered fully. The causes of delinquency are very complex. Some of the experts who study it think it is to be explained by a mixture of heredity, environment, social status, and mental health. But sociologists have succeeded in identifying at least some of the characteristics and circumstances peculiar to boys and girls who offend against the law.

A survey of junior high students in Kansas showed that most teen-age thieves have some features in common which, at the same time, distinguish them from more law-abiding age-mates. Dr. Robert A. Dentler, a sociologist, and Dr. Lawrence J. Monroe, a psychologist, who made the survey together, found that students who admitted stealing also confessed they were not getting along well with their parents. And they described patterns of leisure time activity which were more or less the same for all of them.

In the study, 912 boys and girls were chosen from three different junior high schools, in a suburban, a farm, and a rural non-farm community. They were first asked several questions about stealing:

1. Have you ever taken little things (worth less than $2) that did not belong to you?

2. Have you ever taken things of value (worth between $2 and $50)?

3. Have you ever taken things from someone's desk or locker at school without his permission?

4. Have you ever taken a car without the owner's knowledge?

5. Have you ever taken things of great value (over $50)?

* See "How Much Delinquency Is There?" in this book.

These were questions taken from a questionnaire which had been drawn up previously by F. Ivan Nye and James F. Short, Jr., of Washington State University and given to high school students. But Dentler and Monroe were guided by the fact that most young offenders launch upon their delinquencies between the ages of nine and twelve and they chose their sample of students from the seventh and eighth grades of the three junior high schools.

Of course, the usefulness of the study depended on the truthfulness of the students. However, the teen-agers were not required to give their names and any who were guilty seemed quite willing to admit it on the questionnaire.

On the basis of their answers to the questions about stealing, the students' behavior was classified as, *No Theft* (if the respondent did not answer "yes" to any question); or *Some Theft* (1 or 2 "yeses" in the answers); or *High Theft* (3 to 5 "yeses" in the answers).

As might be expected, 529 students claimed they had never stolen anything. Another 304 students admitted stealing some things sometimes. And a much smaller number—only 79 out of 912—confessed to stealing many times or things of great value.

> Once we broke into old man Petri's store and took some cigarettes and candy. But the best time was when we found that summer cottage all boarded up for the season. The guy left his liquor cabinet stocked, so we just helped ourselves. And we took the TV set for our hangout.

Not the facts of stealing but the reasons for it were what interested the sociologists. They wondered how Jerry's background or his past experiences made him different from other students who did not steal.

So, the research team sifted through the basic personal characteristics which each student supplied in the questionnaire, to find possible correlations between reported stealing and sex, age, school grade, place of residence, father's occupation, father's education, order of birth (was the student the eldest or youngest child in a family?), and other background information (Table 1).

Only three of the personal characteristics seemed to have any relation to stealing.

TABLE 1

Correlation of Theft with Social and Personal Characteristics

SOCIAL AND PERSONAL CHARACTERISTICS	No THEFT (N: 529)	SOME THEFT (N: 304)	HIGH THEFT (N: 79) *
1) Sex:			
% Male	37%	61%	67%
% Female	63	39	33
2) Age:			
% 14 & over	13	17	25
% 13	48	52	50
% 12 & under	39	31	25
3) Grade:			
% Seventh	54	50	53
% Eighth	46	50	47
4) Birth Order:			
% Youngest	18	16	24
% Oldest	44	43	28
% Other	38	41	48
5) Family:			
% Broken	6	5	11
% Complete	94	95	89
6) Father's Occupation:			
% High status	23	25	12
% Middle status	25	30	34
% Low status	52	45	54
7) Father's Education:			
% College	28	27	34
% H. S. grad.	31	33	23
% Less than H. S. grad.	41	40	43
8) Community: †			
% Suburban	58	33	9
% Urban fringe	54	38	8
% Small town	62	31	7

* N means the number of students in the group.
† Percentages total 100 percent for the characteristics numbered 1 to 7. But in Number 8 they do not total 100 percent because the figures are from the three localities.

First, boys were much more likely to report stealing than girls. In fact, almost 67 percent of those classified as High Theft and 61 percent of those in the Some Theft class were boys. In the No Theft class, 2 out of every 3 were girls.

Second, stealing was more often reported by older students, especially those over 14. At the same time, however, there was no difference between the general rates of stealing for seventh and eighth graders. Thus, the two sociologists assumed that the higher rates of stealing among older students probably came from 15- and 16-year-olds who had been held back in the lower grades.

Third, students who were the youngest in a family seemed more likely to report stealing than those who were the first-born.

Strangely enough, no notable correlations were found between stealing and broken homes, or the size of the student's family, or his father's education and occupation, or even where the family lived, whether in the suburbs or the small town. In other words, some of the usual reasons given for delinquency—parents who are divorced, those with little education, and those with lower-class backgrounds seemed to have nothing to do with stealing on the part of Kansas teen-agers.

But the students also had been asked to provide information about their personal habits, their home lives, and their leisure time activities. When their answers were matched with reports of stealing, the scientific team found many significant correlations (Table 2).

For example, the students who reported high rates of stealing often also reported not getting along well with their parents. In fact, of all three groups, the High Theft class had the highest proportion which reported they did not confide in their fathers and mothers. The "generation gap" was apparent.*

> Who can talk to your old man? You think he wants to hear about what I'm doing? All he ever says is "Shut up!" or "Do your homework." Neither he or my mother cares about me. All they worry about is my sister. She gets anything she wants. I

* See "Social Change and Parent-Youth Conflict" in *Life in Families* in this *Readings in Sociology* Series.

TABLE 2

Correlation of Theft with Family Characteristics

FAMILY CHARACTERISTICS	No THEFT (N: 529)	SOME THEFT (N: 304)	HIGH THEFT (N: 79)
1) Confiding in Mothers:			
% Much	21%	8%	10%
% Average	62	71	56
% Not confiding	17	21	34
2) Confiding in Fathers:			
% Much	12	7	8
% Average	58	57	41
% Not confiding	30	36	51
3) Obedience:			
% Very obedient	8	2	6
% Average obedient	86	87	67
% Very disobedient	6	11	27
4) Treatment:			
% Very fair	78	71	69
% Generally equal	14	12	17
% Unfair	8	17	14
5) Working Mothers:			
% Full-time work	23	24	24
% Part-time work	9	9	8
% Not employed	68	67	68

don't get anything. So I say the hell with them! They don't pay any attention to me, so I'm not going to pay any attention to them. What do they know, anyhow? They're old. They don't know what kids today like to do.

Of the High Theft students, 27 percent admitted being "very disobedient" to their parents; a strong contrast to the 6 percent in the No Theft category who said they were "very disobedient." But more important, perhaps, the High Theft group claimed their families did not love or care about them. And many felt they were "getting a raw deal at home," or that they were treated unfairly in comparison with their brothers and sisters.

This Kansas inquiry challenged some widely believed myths. For instance, surprisingly, resentment and a sense of being neglected seemed to have little to do with having a mother who was away from home during the day. For many years people have claimed that working mothers have delinquent children largely because they are not at home. The Kansas study found no evidence to support this popular notion.

Another common belief, discounted by the Kansas study, was that students who steal must be less religious than other teenagers. Although the study could not probe the deeper feelings of the High Theft students, it found they at least reported going to church or Sunday School just as regularly as anyone else.

> Sure, I go to church on Sunday. I guess everybody does. Anyhow, my old man makes me go.

Research has shown that three out of four Kansas teen-agers go to church every Sunday, in any case. Of course, this high rate of church attendance may be just peculiar to Kansas and may not really represent trends in other parts of the country.

A third popular mistake is the belief that teen-agers who steal or cause trouble are not liked by their classmates or not picked as "student leaders." The teen-age thief is generally supposed to be an "underachiever," a poor student, and an outcast. The Kansas study found just the opposite:

> My gang runs that school. We make the rules for the other kids. Sure, most of the kids like me. Last year I was elected the Junior Red Cross rep. from my homeroom and I'm co-captain of the Junior High basketball team.

Although High Theft students were sometimes called bullies or fighters by their classmates, most were well liked and more often were considered members of the "leading crowd" at the school than were those in the other two groups. Indeed, many of the High Theft teen-agers actually ranked as class leaders. Either their classmates did not know about the stealing or it did not make any difference, in their minds.

At least the leisure time activities reported by High Theft students matched the popular notion of how so-called delinquents spend their time. Almost three times as many High Theft students as students in the groups that did little or no stealing reported hanging around local soda shops, skating rinks, and street corners as often as three times a week. The High Theft students also reported spending much less time at home, either for studying or just relaxing. And, compared with the No Theft students, almost twice as many High Theft teen-agers went to the movies at least once a week.

> Most of the time I hang out at Richard's Soda Shop on Pine Street. Sometimes we go over to the skating rink. A lot of kids drop in there. You meet some girls or fool around or go back over to Richard's for a Coke. There's a pool hall on Jersey Street where I hang around, too. But you gotta be sixteen to play. 'Course, there's always the movies. I go a couple times a week. . . Home? I stay away as much as possible!

Interestingly, watching television was too universal an activity to prove anything. Almost every teen-ager watched it every day. Besides, even television's critics must admit that it keeps children at home and off the streets.

The most striking discovery of the Kansas study was the correlation between theft and other kinds of delinquency:

> I guess I was just born to get into trouble. I've been down in the Principal's office so many times, he's got a special chair just for me. Last month, my father had to come in and see him about me skipping school. And last year I got caught stuffing paper in the johns so they'd overflow. It was just a joke, but everybody got all hot about it. Most other times it's just been for fighting in the halls or messing around in class.

Almost every High Theft student admitted to at least one other act of unapproved or illegal behavior (Table 3). Many had been truants from school, or driven without a license, or destroyed property. Others had run away from home. The *lowest* percentage claiming they *never* had engaged in any of the six types of misconduct shown in Table 3 are to be found in the High Theft class.

But very few of even the High Theft students had committed such serious acts as burglary. In fact, of serious offenses, only vandalism and illegal driving were mentioned by more than 50 percent of the High Theft students. And roughly two-thirds re-

TABLE 3

Correlation of Theft with Other Types of Misconduct

Type of Misconduct	No Theft	Some Theft	High Theft
1) Vandalism:			
% 3–5 times	1%	5%	15%
% 1–2 times	17	39	47
% Never	82	56	38
2) Driving Without License:			
% 3 or more times	3	3	15
% 1–2 times	22	27	38
% Never	75	70	47
3) Truancy:			
% 3 or more times	1	3	20
% 1–2 times	7	18	23
% Never	92	79	57
4) Gang Fighting:			
% 3 or more times	1	1	16
% 1–2 times	7	13	23
% None	92	86	61
5) Running Away from Home:			
% 3 or more times	2	5	13
% 1–2 times	8	13	20
% Never	90	82	67
6) Breaking and Entering Locked Stores:			
% 3 or more times	0	0	3
% 1–2 times	1	5	18
% Never	99	95	79

ported they had never run away from home or fought in a gang war or seriously injured anyone.

Yet the evidence is still clear: Students who report having stolen repeatedly also report significantly more of other forms of misbehavior as well. Often a career of misbehavior dates back to when the doer was 9 or 10 years old.

The two social scientists were especially interested in the discovery that the High Theft group specialized, though to a limited extent, in certain other offenses, namely vandalism and illegal driving, to which 63 percent and 53 percent confessed, respectively. But the figures on vandalism and illegal driving for the No Theft group were only 18 percent and 25 percent, respectively, and for the Some Theft group, 44 percent and 30 percent. To the sociologist this suggests that if a student belongs in the High Theft class, it may be predicted that he is more likely than the others to be guilty of vandalism and illegal driving.

Unfortunately, the Kansas study, despite its tempting suggestions, cannot definitely state the precise reasons for juvenile delinquency. Although teen-age theft seems linked to unhappy home lives, a history of misbehavior, and wasted leisure time, none of these conditions can be called the cause of delinquency. For, a child who plays hooky does not necessarily become a delinquent. Or he may dislike his family but he does not necessarily turn to stealing.

Yet just the discovery of a pattern that links repeated stealing with vandalism and illegal driving may be one key to the cause; for evidently whatever brings the teen-ager to frequent stealing is a part of the background of his other delinquent acts. The correlation between stealing and other behavior at least offers some additional clues to understanding the differences between teen-agers who are delinquents and others who are not.

Some of the clues are as sad as they are revealing. The two Kansas sociologists learned that "Jerry Bruckner" and many other High Theft students do not think very well of themselves. Indeed, it is plain that they are deeply unhappy. When asked, "Do you like your looks just the way they are?" or "Do you think you are really well liked?" many of them can only answer, "No." They wish desperately to be "better looking" or to have "closer" friends. Jerry's wish was the saddest of all:

> Oh, I look all right, I guess. But sometimes I wish I was someone else living a thousand miles away with a new family. I wish I was somebody people could be proud of.

Sociologists and psychologists must continue to look for the reasons why youngsters steal. But they do know that any steps that are taken to stop, before it is too late, teen-agers who are getting set on a dangerous course must include measures to build up their pride and self-esteem.

Stealing Cars*

How does the boy who steals cars differ from other delinquents who commit other kinds of crimes?

Does he come from a different environment?

What is his cultural, economic, or family background?

After imprisonment will he be likely to rejoin society as a productive member, or as a hardened criminal?

ARREST REPORT: 3RD PRECINCT: 11:45 P.M. July 17. 114 Schuyler Blvd.

Station 3 Patrolmen Hines and Miller responded to report of a speeding auto while in Car 3–1. Proceeded to Young and 14th Streets where auto matching description of a stolen vehicle was spotted and pursued. Pursuit continued for ten blocks at speeds up to 85 miles an hour. Auto went out of control and hit an abutment after making turn onto Schuyler Blvd. Auto found to match description of car stolen in Greendale section lot that same date. Four juveniles, three males and one female, apprehended and booked on grand larceny—auto theft. All four appeared in Juvenile Court, July 18. Female (14) received warning. Two juvenile males (14 and 15) were placed on probation for one year. One juvenile male placed for an indeterminate period at Training School for Boys.

Signed .   .   .   .
Samuel Miller
Arresting Officer

Entry from a police blotter: cold, unfeeling, unemotional, factual. Just another auto theft, just another arrest, just another boy headed for jail—or, perhaps, for a career of crime.

---

* Based in part on "Boys Who Steal Cars" by Erwin Schepses, *Federal Probation*, Vol. 25 (March 1961), pp. 56–62. Reprinted by permission.

According to statistics of the Federal Bureau of Investigation, auto thefts now account for almost 20 percent of all the grand larcenies in the United States. Over half of these auto thefts are committed by young people under 18 years of age.

Unfortunately, neither the dry statistics of the FBI's annual crime index or the colorless reports of the nation's police blotters can answer the questions often asked by sociologists, criminologists, and law-enforcement officials: What kind of boy steals cars?

THE WARWICK BOYS

To answer some of the questions about what kind of boys steal cars—and why they do it—a group of delinquents sentenced to the New York Training School for Boys at Warwick, New York (better known simply as "Warwick"), were studied over a three-year period. The study was made by Erwin Schepses, the Director of Social Service at the institution.

At the time of the study, Warwick admitted boys between the ages of 12 and 16 who had been sentenced by courts in New York City and rural Orange County where the school is located.

From the total of 1,408 boys admitted in the three-year period, Dr. Schepses placed in a group for study 81 boys with records of one or more auto thefts. As a comparison or "control" group, another 81 delinquent boys who had committed other types of delinquency—general theft including shoplifting, assault, or vandalism—were selected by Schepses at random. However, he made sure that the control group was divided into the same proportions racially and ethnically as the rest of the school, that is, 33 whites (41 percent), 36 blacks (45 percent), and 12 Puerto Ricans (15 percent).

For the background information he needed for measuring differences between the auto thieves and the other types of delinquents, Dr. Schepses turned to the court records and the reports of probation officers, social workers, and others who knew the boys before they came to Warwick. To this information he added the evaluation of the school psychiatrist, the results of intelligence, achievement, and personality tests, plus the reports of various teachers, supervisors, and staff members who knew the boys after they entered the training school.

After release, court records of any new offenses committed by the boys were forwarded to the training school so the Warwick staff could keep track of their former charges in the outside world.

Thus, Dr. Schepses and his research team were provided with data on the boys "before," "during," and "after."

Even before starting the study, the officials at the training school noticed that the 81 teen-age auto thieves could be divided into two smaller groups: the "pure thieves" who had committed no crimes other than auto theft (22 boys), and the "mixed thieves" who combined auto theft with various other kinds of delinquent behavior (59 boys). These two sub-groups often differed as much from each other as they did from the control group of other delinquents.

WHY BOYS STEAL CARS

For the Warwick car thieves—both the pure and the mixed, the main reason for stealing a car was simply to have a good time —to take a "joy ride." Only eight of the boys had used a stolen car as a means of escape from home, or an institution, or from some other situation they found intolerable. And none of the boys used a stolen car in connection with another crime, such as a holdup or an attack on a girl or woman. Of course, the Warwick boys were relatively young, so major crimes or sexual adventures may not have entered their minds.

The Warwick car thefts seemed more like the typical, senseless stunts of boys showing off to impress their friends, especially since the majority of cases involved two or more boys. Only four boys actually stole cars by themselves—and all four had been making so-called "escapes," that is, trying to run away.

Solely from this evidence, teen-agers' car thefts appear to be group activities. Perhaps it is not surprising, then, that many sociologists find that adolescent car thieves usually get along better with their fellow teen-agers than other types of delinquents.

Is there a common denominator, a single reason, for all adolescent car theft? Some research workers argue that the teen-agers who are auto thieves come from middle-class or working-class homes where the mothers are overpowering and the fathers are pushed into the background. Boys from such homes, say the sociologists, fight against identifying themselves with their mothers (or any women), and try to assert their masculinity by stealing cars.

This theory may be true of some boys, but the Warwick study revealed that adolescent auto theft is more likely to have been caused by a complex combination of many reasons than by any one reason. At least the youthful offenders at Warwick came from an almost unlimited variety of backgrounds: homes where the father ruled with an iron hand and homes where the father was always absent; well-to-do homes and poverty-stricken homes; broken homes and apparently happy homes. Some of the case histories demonstrate the diversity of backgrounds.

Salvatore: one of 16 children born to illiterate parents of Italian descent. His father has a court record and so do several of his older brothers. Began to steal at age 13 with other boys. Below average intelligence. Reads at fourth grade level. Apparently a mentally limited boy who has turned to crime because of his poor environment.

George: black, illegitimate, abandoned by his mother and raised by his father and a "stepmother." Average intelligence. Steals with a companion thought to be a homosexual. Stealing and other delinquent acts are apparently connected with sexual problems, particularly his difficulty in finding a model of male identity.

Sam: a Polish-Jewish refugee from Nazi persecution, both parents killed when he was a small child. Lived with various friends and relatives until finally went on his own at the age of 11. Lived in the streets, sleeping in alleys and empty buildings. Average intelligence. Also shrewd and calculating with little awareness of any moral or ethical standards except his own pleasure and comfort. Apparently this boy is so hardened by his experiences that he can feel no remorse or guilt over any criminal act. Car theft is just another attack on a society he hates.

Henry: the only son of a well-to-do draftsman of German descent. High intelligence but disturbed over home life. Stole an auto and was apprehended many miles from his home. Even after his term in the training school, he refused to return home.

For this boy, stealing a car is an expression of adolescent rebellion.

In addition to the vast number of individual reasons for car theft among teen-agers, the Warwick study revealed many broad and more general cultural reasons that may affect all youth.

In the first place, the United States is a motorized nation where even three-car families are common. Almost every American is fascinated by cars. More important, the car has become a tangible symbol of the adult power, prestige, and freedom that many teen-agers so badly desire.

Also, Americans of all ages are constantly bombarded by advertising inviting them to "Tame a Cougar!" "Hop into a Mustang!" "Get away in a Barracuda!" or "Grab a Charger!" For some impressionable adolescents, the combination of constant sales pitch and natural fascination is simply too much. Instead of waiting to make a $500 down payment, some teen-agers simply grab *somebody else's* Charger!

In addition, the mere act of operating a big machine at high speeds is a thrill in itself. Moreover, an automobile satisfies the teen-ager's natural restlessness and fulfills his craving to keep moving from place to place. Besides, a car can get a teen-ager away from his parents, school teachers, police, and all other prying, snooping adult eyes.

Finally, there is a sexual element in many car thefts. For younger boys, stealing a car impresses the girls. For older boys, a stolen car provides the perfect, private, isolated spot for forbidden adventures.

WHAT KIND OF BOYS STEAL CARS?

Although there seem to be several reasons why *any boy* might be tempted to steal a car, the Warwick study showed that a *certain type of boy* is more likely to commit the actual crime.

RACIAL DIFFERENCES

For example, 59 percent of the Warwick car thieves were white, 32 percent were black, and 9 percent were Puerto Rican. By contrast, the control group of boys, whose racial make-up matched that of the school, contained only 41 percent whites, plus 45 percent blacks and 15 percent Puerto Ricans.

Within the "pure" group of auto thieves who had stolen only cars, the percentage of white boys was even higher—nearly 60 percent! (A similar study of slightly older delinquents in Detroit revealed that 230 out of 260 boys arrested for auto theft were white—or 88 percent!)

Why is car theft a white boy's crime? Many police like to claim that black teen-agers avoid stealing cars simply because they know they would attract too much attention behind the wheel of a stolen auto. However, if, as is likely, the social and economic backgrounds of the teen-agers influence their stealing habits, then car theft can be interpreted as a white, middle-class crime.

Socioeconomic Background

The Warwick boys involved in car thefts generally enjoyed much better social status and economic security than boys in the control group. Indeed, almost 40 percent of the "pure" auto thieves came from comfortable, even wealthy middle-class families which could afford to spend money on luxuries after the basic essentials of food, clothing, rent, and utilities had been bought. Another 45 percent of the "pure" thieves came from homes which at least had enough money for the basic essentials. Only one boy in the "pure" group came from a welfare family.

On the other hand, 22 percent of the boys in both the "mixed" theft and control groups came from welfare homes.

Obviously, the connection between the relatively higher social and economic status of most youthful car thieves and the relatively low number of black thieves is very real. The white middle-class teen-ager simply is more often exposed to cars in his own family and in his neighborhood. As a result, he is probably more car conscious and probably learns to drive much earlier than black boys from the slums. Ironically, even in crime, black Americans are disadvantaged and lacking in opportunities!

Family Background

The true emotional climate of a delinquent's home is difficult to determine because the sociologist must depend on the word of the boys themselves. However, it is possible to note if a teenager's home life is broken or disturbed by the absence of one or both parents.

Among the Warwick boys in the "pure" group, only 40 percent came from broken homes. The mixed group of thieves was slightly worse off, with 58 percent coming from broken homes. Obviously, the boys arrested for car theft—especially those who had committed no other crimes—came from much more secure, and possibly happier, homes than other delinquents.

AGE OF ARREST

As a rule, the boys in the group of "pure" thieves started their delinquent careers relatively later than other delinquents. The typical "pure" auto thief was over 14 before he stole his first auto. However, almost one third of the other delinquents already were seasoned delinquents by age 14.

INTELLIGENCE

The "pure" auto thieves were generally smarter than other delinquents. The tests showed that less than 10 percent of the "pure" thieves at Warwick were of only borderline intelligence or were mentally deficient.

By contrast, close to 30 percent of both the mixed thieves and the control group had IQ's below 80 and thus had less than average mentality.

Poor reading skill was a trait of all three groups of boys. However, almost 50 percent of the "pure" thieves still could read above the sixth-grade level. But among the mixed group only 32 percent, and among the control group only 28 percent could do so. Moreover, only 18 percent of the "pure" group could be considered *nonreaders*, that is, below third-grade level. Over 30 percent of the mixed group and nearly 40 percent of the control group fell into this category.

AFTER WARWICK

After leaving Warwick, a boy usually kept in contact with the school through after-care programs until either he had made a good adjustment in the community, or had been committed to another correctional institution, or had been placed on probation by an adult court. Of course, some boys became separated from Warwick by joining the armed services or moving with their families out of the state.

The adjustment of a boy to institutional life after his arrest seemed to have little connection with his type of crime. In other words, teen-age car thieves behaved no better or no worse than any other boys behind bars.

Once on the outside, however, the "pure" auto thieves did quite well. Forty-five percent of them made a good adjustment to normal society—which is considerably better than either the group of mixed thieves or the control group. However, another 45 percent of the "pure" group soon found themselves back in trouble again—the majority of them for auto theft.

CONCLUSIONS

If Warwick boys are typical of young delinquents between the ages of 12 and 16, then car theft seems a "group crime," committed mainly for thrills, or for fun, or to show off. Occasionally, stolen cars may be used to escape from a home or an unhappy situation, but they are used rarely in the commission of other offenses.

Although there seems to be no common denominator, or single overwhelming reason, for car thefts by young boys, the delinquents who steal cars are a certain type, distinct from the boys who commit other crimes such as general theft, assault, and vandalism.

Statistically, at least, teen-age car thieves—especially those who steal only cars and nothing else—are usually (1) white, (2) older, (3) brighter, (4) better readers, (5) of higher social and economic status, and (6) the children of more secure homes. Knowing this much about them is only a first step on the way to discovering the reason for car theft. We still do not know how to explain the fact that when the "pure" auto thief gets into trouble again, it is usually for stealing another car.

Cell 202: Who Will Come Back?*

What kind of problems do ex-offenders face when they are released from prison and seek to re-establish themselves in the free community?

Does the notion of "straightening up" imply one type of acceptable adjustment only, or is it consistent with a variety of types of adjustment? If the latter, then what are some of the different ways in which ex-offenders may "straighten up" or revert to crime?

How do modes of adjustment on release from prison vary with the type of community to which released offenders return?

What does it mean for the work of parole officers and others who wish to assist released offenders, that offenders tend to "straighten up" or revert to crime in ways closely related to the community to which they return?

Stan Wybocki and Peter Gianno had shared Cell 202 at Hillsboro State Prison for almost two years. Spending much of their day in an iron-barred cubicle containing two bunks, a sink, and an open toilet, the men had devoted most of their conversation to prison gossip—who had cigarettes or narcotics, who had "ratted" on whom. Now the subject of their discussions had changed, because both men were due to be released from Hillsboro in the coming week. How would they make out once the prison doors had shut behind them? Would they be able to stay out of jail, or would one or both of them return?

The occupants of Cell 202 had much in common. Both had been sent to prison for an offense against property. Stan had been

---

* Adapted from "Reformation and Recidivism Among Italian and Polish Criminal Offenders" by Harold Finestone, *American Journal of Sociology* (The University of Chicago Press), Vol. 72, No. 6 (May 1967), pp. 575–588. Reprinted by permission.

part of a car theft ring which operated in a nearby city, and Peter had been convicted on several counts of grand larceny. Neither man was married, although both had steady girlfriends who visited them weekly. Sunday, when inmates could receive callers, was extremely important to the men—a time at which contacts with the outside world were kept alive.

It was on visiting day, however, that the two men who shared Cell 202 appeared strikingly different. Peter's afternoon hours were filled with family and friends bearing gossip and food. Stan, on the other hand, seldom had callers other than his girl and his parents.

As the time of their release drew closer, both Stan and Peter spoke of their concern with "getting a good job," although Peter's conversation was generously sprinkled with references to his "connections." Peter also talked about the party which his family was having on the night of his release, and he told of the offers made by the various members of his neighborhood of money, room, and company. During Peter's enthusiastic description of the life which lay outside of the prison walls, Stan was uncomfortable and silent. He was not even sure that his parents would be glad to see him.

On Monday, Stan Wybocki was released and returned to the Polish neighborhood in which he had been raised. On the following Thursday, Peter was met by his Italian brothers at the prison gates and driven home to the party he had confidently described to Stan. Thus each man moved from the harsh, regulated life of prison into the ethnic environment from which he had come.

How well would each adjust to his freedom?

Would Stan and Peter move into conventional roles?

Or would their different cultural backgrounds and ethnic settings create different problems for them to solve as they reformed their lives?

Since punishment and rehabilitation are a big and controversial part of the problems of crime, social scientists have been interested in the fate of men like Stan and Peter. Recognizing that most released offenders return to the environment from which they were sent to prison, Harold Finestone, a sociologist at the

University of Minnesota, concentrated his attention on two specific ethnic groups—the Italians and the Poles—to learn about the influences which might affect a man's rehabilitation or return to crime.

First, however, Finestone suggested that *any* discussion of crime and reformation had to be preceded by a basic assumption about the nature of criminality. One supposition might be, for example, that the tendency towards crime is like a cancer whose evil effect on an individual can only be removed by radical changes in the person's character or environment. An alternate theory, and the one on which Finestone based his study, is that a criminal career is marked by frequent returns to noncriminal behavior, and rehabilitation consists of a constant offering of choices between noncriminal and criminal activities.

Armed, then, with this assumption about the possibilities of reformation, Finestone's next step was to gain an understanding of some of the environments in which released offenders choose either to "go straight" or to break the law again.

Since his study was focused on two specific ethnic groups, Finestone had to be very careful in selecting the men whose progress he would examine. Using the resources of the Chicago Area Project and the Illinois State Penitentiary System, he was able to study a sample of 54 men who fulfilled the following requirements:

1. *Ethnicity*. (a) The father of all offenders should be foreign-born; (b) prior to their first commitment to prison, all offenders should have lived in an ethnic neighborhood.

2. *Criminality*. All offenders should have been imprisoned for an offense against property: robbery, burglary, or larceny.

3. *Age* (at the time of first commitment to prison). All offenders should have been committed to prison for the first time on or prior to the age of 21.

4. *Recidivists* (meaning "those who relapse or return"). Recidivists were those offenders who had been returned to prison for a second time, either for violation of parole or for the commission of a new crime within five years of their first release from prison.

Having selected the men in terms of ethnic group, age, offense, and recidivism (Table 1), Finestone interviewed his sub-

TABLE 1
Distribution of Inmates by Ethnicity and Recidivism

	First Offenders	Recidivists	Total
Italians	11	19	30
Poles	10	14	24
Total	21	33	54

jects. He wanted to find out what characteristics of each ethnic community accounted for the kinds of problems encountered by Italian and Polish offenders after they were released from prison. Was reform easier in one setting than in another? Was recidivism, or return to crime, more likely in one ethnic group than in the other?

In search of data, Finestone first turned his attention to the Polish neighborhood, and watched men like Stan Wybocki struggle with what seemed to be their most serious problem—that of gaining acceptance within the community. As Stan's lonely Sunday afternoons had suggested, there was a marked difference between the tolerance of criminality shown by the Poles and that shown by the Italians. Comparing the relative frequency of visits received by Polish and Italian inmates during 18 months in prison, Finestone recognized early a clue to the fact that Polish families were far less able to accept deviant behavior than were the Italians. Italian prisoners received more than twice as many visits from various members of their families as did the Poles (Table 2).

Looking more closely at the specific characteristics of Polish families in America, Finestone saw that whether a Polish offender was married or single seemed to be most important in determining if he would reform or, instead, return to crime. Eight out of ten Polish one-time offenders had been married during the post-release period as compared with 4 out of 15 of those who went back to jail a second time.

The fact that a Pole's success as a husband and father was so significant in his rehabilitation is not surprising in light of the

TABLE 2
Visitors to Inmates, by Ethnicity

Visitors and Number of Visits	Italians	Poles
Parents:		
Total	769	311
Average	12	5
Brothers and Sisters:		
Total	579	310
Average	9	5
Other Relatives:		
Total	341	117
Average	5	2
All Relatives:		
Total	1689	738
Average	26	11

structure of the Polish-American community. Of all the social institutions among Poles in the United States, the *nuclear* family—husband, wife, and children—has proven itself to be the most stable. The *extended* family system, found in Poland, did not survive the crossing to America, and Finestone was able to establish that a released Polish offender was best able to gain the approval of his community by forming and supporting his own family. Thus, Stan Wybocki's decision to marry his girl as soon as possible will, as indicated by Finestone's research, be a demonstration of his determination and personal independence, qualities valued by the Polish community.

Interestingly, Polish men often thought they were satisfying the same values when they engaged in an activity which seemed to characterize those Polish offenders who return to prison—heavy drinking. Marriage and drunkenness—sometimes the two together —appeared to offer two alternatives by which released Polish offenders attempted to gain acceptance in their community. Since drinking among immigrants had generally offered a lonely man a substitute for the family atmosphere, Polish offenders of the second generation extended the idea so that, for some men, excessive social drinking could be as expressive of individuality as marriage itself.

Not surprisingly, descriptions by Polish recidivists of their return to crime are almost always characterized by repeated references to drinking.

We went to this tavern on the way home. It was cold out. We had a few drinks there and we got to talking to this guy and we asked him if he wanted to go to some other place. So we were walking and the next thing I knew we had him in the alley and I hit him and we took his money and that was it. We didn't discuss it or anything. It just happened that way. We went into another tavern and were drinking and that's where the police caught us. The guy had told them we were both intoxicated and the cops took a chance. There were only a few places open at 2:30 A.M. and they found us. We denied it. They found his watch on us and that was it and I was on my way back here. We had enough money to drink, but on the way somehow we got him in the alley. I was drunk, because if I knew that I had stolen anything I would have gotten away. Here I was in a tavern a few blocks away. I can't explain that. After we sobered up at the police station we said, "What did we do that for?"

A third influence affecting the reformation of a Polish offender was honest employment. Here Finestone discovered that there was little difference between released offenders who were successfully rehabilitated and those who were not—most men in either group had conventional, legitimate jobs and most Polish men did not seriously consider alternatives to honest employment. In their semiskilled and unskilled occupations, Poles of the second generation were not far removed from the outlook of their fathers, who regarded working as an obligation that was almost religious.

It was in examining the role of employment in the rehabilitation of the released Polish offender that Finestone discovered the most striking difference between them and their Italian counterparts. While the gaining and holding of an acceptable job seemed to be relatively easy for Stan Wybocki, the problem of finding honest work was apparently Peter Gianno's most serious hurdle. For the recently released Italian offender, the maintaining of legal employment was complicated by circumstances found in the Italian community.

First, unlike the Poles, the Italians were very much concerned with the rewards of their efforts. Many men within their ethnic community were noticeably wealthy, which made it hard for others to be satisfied with the often menial pay they could earn at honest jobs.

Second, because of its preoccupation with the money earned as well as with the job itself, the Italian community did not disapprove of certain kinds of work which are frowned upon by others.* That is, Peter was faced with the possibility of work which was thought *amoral* by the Italians, but which might be regarded as *illegal* by the rest of society.

Finally, Italian offenders were often subjected to strong pressure from friends in the criminal world to engage in profitable, illegal business. Even as he reported for his job in a local machine shop, Peter was constantly tempted by offers from his friends to make three times as much money as a runner for the local numbers game.†

Closely associated with the problem of finding and keeping honest work was the influence of the informal peer group in the Italian community on the released offender. From one point of view, the street-corner society in which Peter had grown up offered him a warm, hospitable group within which to reform his life. In contrast to the Poles, whose communities in American cities were structured very like their parish system in Europe, the Italians had transplanted few of their social institutions other than the family. Thus to fill this social vacuum there had emerged what was to be the organizing element of Italian-American communities—the informal street-corner association of young male adults of the second generation. These street-corner groups and their leaders became the essential units in the hierarchies of power which controlled politics and the rackets.‡

* See "What Is Delinquent Behavior?" in this book.
† See "The Slum: Opportunities for Crime and Delinquency" in this book.
‡ See "Age-Mates: The World of the French Child" in *Life in Families* in this *Reading in Sociology* Series.

For Peter Gianno, then, the peer group (his friends) exercised a pressure on his rehabilitation which was absent from Stan Wybocki's experience. Although Peter had more channels through which to re-enter community life, he also had to contend with a greater number of possibly criminal associations.

Once having established that the values and organization of two ethnic settings presented different problems for men returning from prison, Finestone turned his attention to features of the Polish and Italian communities which seemed most closely connected with reformation or recidivism.

First, the sociologist recognized a difference between the *quality* and *quantity* of help offered by Polish and Italian families to released offenders. Again reflecting its emphasis on the importance of the nuclear family, Polish tradition made it unlikely that anyone besides a Polish offender's immediate family would offer him either financial or emotional resources. In contrast, the return of the Italian offenders to their ethnic community was turned into a social occasion for the extended family, when aunts, uncles, and cousins gathered together and presented gifts of money and clothing to the kinsman restored to them. Further, Italian families continued their collective responsibility for the offender throughout the post-prison period, offering room and board, financial assistance, and so on. For men like Stan Wybocki, however, there was a seldom expressed but barely concealed tendency for members of the family to dissociate themselves from the offender.

This marked difference in the ways in which Polish and Italian families behave toward relatives who have been released from prison is a reflection, according to Finestone, of a basic contrast in Polish and Italian attitudes towards the nature of man. From evidence gathered from various sources, the sociologist concluded that the Italian ethnic group regarded human nature as a mixture of good and evil, while the Polish ethnic group saw human nature as predominantly evil. Finestone went on from that hypothesis to suggest that the philosophy of the Poles would be accompanied by a rigid moral code which was relatively absent among the Italians.

Applying Finestone's theory to the situation of released offenders, it would appear that an Italian family could be much more tolerant of even criminal behavior than could the Poles. Stan Wybocki's family, for example, would be forced to make an uneasy compromise between their affection for Stan and their disapproval of his actions. Peter's relatives, on the other hand, could welcome his return without feeling it necessary to pass judgment on his past or present behavior.

What did the different ethnic viewpoints on human nature mean in terms of reform and recidivism?

Finestone suggested that while an uncompromising value system offered a Polish offender few alternatives by which to re-enter the community, the fact that clear judgments were made about the "right and wrong" of various activities forced a re-leased offender to commit himself definitely to either lawful or criminal behavior. The Italian neighborhood, on the other hand, with its less strict, more tolerant system of values, offered a re-leased criminal both greater support during his rehabilitation and, at the same time, more opportunity to return to criminal activity.

Based on his analysis of the two ethnic situations, Finestone suggested that to give real help to released offenders the correc-tional program must take into account the environment into which a man will go from prison, as well as his personal and so-cial characteristics. A program which would be appropriate for Stan Wybocki, for example, who will depend largely on his own strength and resources in the face of an indifferent or even hos-tile community, will not necessarily help Peter Gianno, who will return to both law-abiding and criminally oriented groups which will be rivals for his loyalty.

The answer, then, to the question, *Which man will return to Cell 202?* lies somewhere in the complicated, confusing area of reform and rehabilitation. In the work of sociologists like Harold Finestone, society is slowly becoming aware of the need to know more about the pressures and influences which will affect released offenders as they attempt to reshape their lives.

Crime Waves: The Record of
120 Years in Boston*

Are American cities of today really more dangerous for the average citizen than ever before?

What features of the structure of society are associated with crime in our cities?

Why have the rates of some crimes gone up and others gone down over the years?

CITY'S ARRESTS UP 14% IN YEAR:
SHARPEST RISE IS AMONG YOUTHS
—**The New York Times**

COURT RECORDS SHOW HUGE RISE IN
BOSTON CRIME LAST 10 YEARS
—**The Boston Globe**

BOSTON AVERAGED TWO MURDERS A
WEEK IN 1968
—**The Boston Globe**

Newspaper headlines declare crime out of control. Politicians call for law and order. City dwellers complain that they are afraid to go out at night. Student rebellions disrupt our universities. And assassins kill great popular leaders in daylight before crowds of witnesses. Indeed, this seems the Age of Crime.

But are these times really any more violent than earlier days in our history? Are Americans really more criminal now than they were 30, or 50, or even 100 years ago?

---

* Adapted from "The Criminal Patterns of Boston Since 1849" by Theodore N. Ferdinand, *American Journal of Sociology* (The University of Chicago Press), Vol. 73, No. 1 (July 1967), pp. 84–99. Reprinted by permission.

Surprisingly enough, 20th-century Americans seem relatively peace-loving and law-abiding compared with their 19th-century ancestors. Despite the alarming recent rise in crime, a detailed study of police records for the years between 1849 and 1967 shows that the overall crime rate in our cities has *decreased*.

This information is encouraging, of course, but it raises some perplexing questions. First, what has caused the long-term decline in urban crime rates? And, second, if statistics show this trend should continue downward, how can the recent and contradictory rise in crime be explained?

THE INTEREST IN CRIME

Sociologists have found that broad patterns of criminal behavior are often closely associated with major changes in the character and structure of society or with unusual events in national history. The study of long-term criminal behavior in the United States is particularly interesting because few countries have changed so dramatically in so short a time.

Less than 150 years ago, the United States was a nation of farmers. Even large cities like Boston or New York were only marketplaces for the farmlands that surrounded them. Following the Civil War (1861–1865), however, most American cities became busy industrial centers which attracted thousands of immigrants from both nearby farms and countries overseas. Within another 50 years, America had become an urban nation. Today, more than 70 percent of the population is urban.

The record of arrests compiled by police in these cities during the past century can provide a means to trace historical trends in criminal behavior. The police of Boston, Massachusetts, for example, began issuing annual summaries of arrests in 1849. Now the Department of Justice issues crime statistics for all states and calculates a "crime index" for each state and city, based on the local rates for seven major crimes.

Professor Theodore N. Ferdinand, a sociologist at Northeastern University in Boston, correlated criminal behavior reported by the police with the major events and social changes shaping life in Boston between 1849 and 1951—a period in which the city's population grew from 136,000 to 801,000. Crime figures for

1967 have been included to show the more recent patterns in the general trend. In the long run such studies are valuable because, armed with a knowledge of what *has* happened, the sociologist is in a position to predict what *will* happen.

MAJOR CRIME RATES: 1849–1951

From 1875 until 1951, the overall crime rate in Boston, based on the figures on seven major crimes, *declined* almost without interruption (see Figure 1). Since 1951, crime has risen again, but to a level which is still less than half what it was in 1875.

Forgetting for a moment the recent upswing in crime, why did the overall crime rate fall so sharply after 1875? Did Bostonians actually become less criminally inclined as their city grew into a modern metropolis? Or did the attitudes of the courts and police toward crime soften and did they become more lax in dealing with lawbreakers? A look at seven of the most serious crimes may provide an answer.

Murder (Figure 2). The rate of murders in Boston, like the total crime rate, declined steadily during the 100-year period. Since murder is the most serious of crimes, it is unlikely that the police became less vigilant in rounding up killers.

Also, the steady fall of the murder rate seems not to be linked with any specific events in history. Neither great wars nor major depressions had any consistent effect on the number of murders. For example, during the Civil War (1861–1865), murders were fewer, but during the two World Wars (1917–1918 and 1941–1945) they increased again.

The only answer seems to be that Bostonians became less murderous as their city became larger and more cosmopolitan.

Manslaughter (Figure 3). The long-term trend for manslaughter (unplanned killing, as in traffic accidents) follows a much different curve. The manslaughter rate remained about the same from 1849 until 1906, when the number of manslaughter arrests suddenly began rising. Arrests reached a plateau almost six times higher than at any time during the 19th century and remained there for nearly 20 years. But about 1935 the rate of manslaughter arrests began to fall again.

Perhaps the dramatic rise in manslaughter can be linked to the introduction of automobiles on Boston highways. Cars were

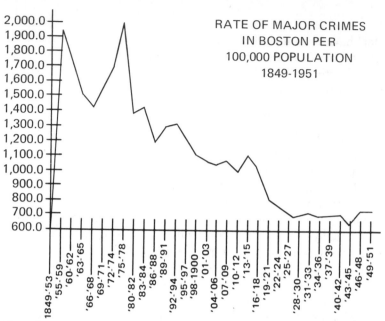

Figure 1. — Rate of major crimes in Boston per 100,000 population, 1849-1951

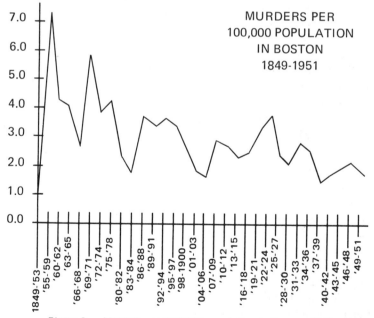

Figure 2. — Murders per 100,000 population in Boston, 1849-1951

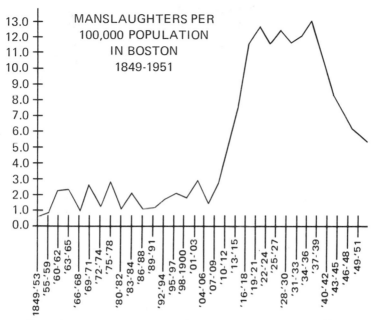

Figure 3. — Manslaughters per 100,000 population in Boston, 1849-1951

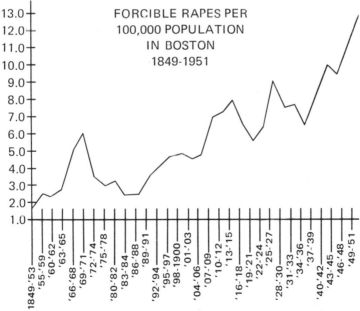

Figure 4. — Forcible rapes per 100,000 population in Boston, 1849-1951

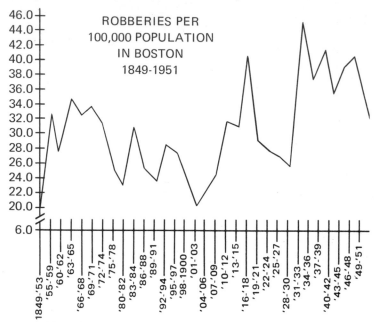

Figure 5. — Robberies per 100,000 population in Boston, 1849-1951

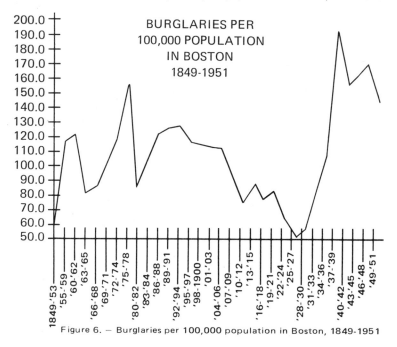

Figure 6. — Burglaries per 100,000 population in Boston, 1849-1951

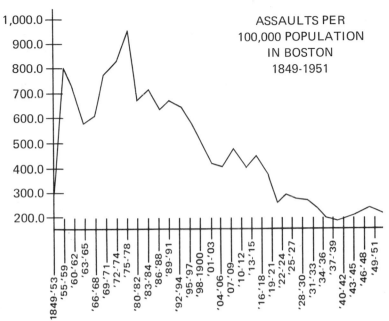

Figure 7. — Assaults per 100,000 population in Boston, 1849-1951

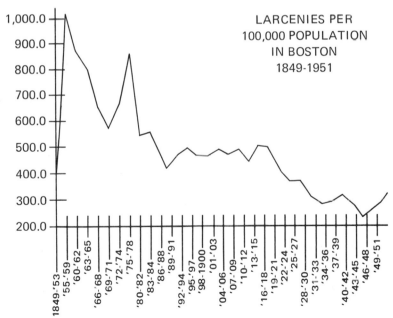

Figure 8. — Larcenies per 100,000 population in Boston, 1849-1951

considered "dangerous," newfangled contraptions and police may have been quick to charge drivers responsible for fatal accidents with manslaughter.

Why, then, did the rate fall off after 1936, when many more cars were on the roads? It may have been that twenty years of driving experience, plus the improved design of both cars and highways, have cut down the actual number of manslaughters by auto. Or perhaps the police just became more stoic about accidents. Or they may have charged drivers with other offenses, such as reckless driving, instead of manslaughter.

Rape (Figure 4). Also unlike the overall crime rate, the number of arrests for forcible rape rose steadily between 1849 and 1951. It appears that the factors which seemed to have the most influence over the rate—depressions and wars—are actually associated with decreases in it. For example, the number of forcible rapes declined during World War I (1917–1918) and the depressions of 1873–1878, 1919–1921, and 1930–1939. By contrast, the number of arrests rose sharply during the prosperous years of 1866–1872, 1906–1915, 1922–1927, and 1940–1951.

The relationship between war and rape may be easily explained, since large numbers of physically able men leave the community during wartime. The effect of depressions is more complicated, but it seems these times create "psychological depression" as well as economic hardship. Men become more interested in preserving or holding onto whatever possessions they already have rather than involving themselves in risky adventures. During more prosperous times, they may lose some of their caution and become more bold and reckless.

The overall rate of forcible rape has been rising despite the minor downward dips during times of war or depression. This upward climb began in 1905, or, again, at about the time the automobile was introduced into American life. Most sociologists agree that the automobile helped revolutionize behavior by allowing young couples to get away from the protective eyes of parents and chaperones. Perhaps this new privacy and intimacy also created dangerous situations which led to sexual crimes.

The rise in the rate of forcible rape also coincides with the growth of the middle class in Boston. Traditionally, middle-class girls have been more likely to report sexual attacks than their lower-class sisters. As more and more of Boston's girls became members of the middle class, the number of *arrests* for this offense may have naturally climbed upward, although the actual number of crimes remained the same.

Robberies (Figure 5). Robbery, that is, a holdup in which the victim is threatened or harmed, follows a pattern almost completely opposite that of rape. Robberies increased very sharply during both World Wars (1917–1918 and 1941–1945) and the Great Depression (1930–1939).

Burglaries (Figure 6). Burglary, that is, theft following breaking into a house or building, followed a pattern similar to robberies, with one exception. The highest burglary rates came during times of economic depression. But the rate did not increase during times of war; indeed Boston's burglary rate declined consistently during all three major wars: between 1849 and 1951 (1861–1865, 1917–1918, and 1941–1945).

Assaults (Figure 7). Boston's police records for assault are particularly interesting because the rate seems to be divided into two separate parts. From 1855 to 1924, the assault rate seems to respond to all major national events, usually rising each time there was a war and in the depressions of 1872 and 1907. After 1924, however, none of these events seemed to have any effect on the rate, which dropped steadily until 1940.

This strange pattern may reflect changes in police attitudes more than anything else. Simple assault can range from screaming a threat at a person on the street to punching someone in the nose during a barroom argument. Almost anyone might be guilty of "simple assault," and aggressive behavior of that sort tends to increase during times of crisis. Possibly the 19th-century police were much more diligent in tracking down and solving every case of minor crime, and so the bulk of the assault arrests probably were for "simple assault," or the type of crime which increases in times of stress.

By contrast, the overworked modern policemen usually cannot attempt to track down and bring to trial every barroom brawler except in those particular incidents which result in serious injury to the victim. Thus, major, or aggravated, assault cases probably make up the greater part of the arrests after 1925. And, judging by the records, aggravated assault, like murder, seemed unaffected by public events. In other words, serious violence became less widespread as the city grew in size.

Larceny (Figure 8). The rate of larcenies (thefts) in Boston followed a pattern similar to that of assaults. Again, the pattern is split in two, with the rate responding to all major events until about 1887 and after that responding to none at all. Strangely enough, the Great Depression (1930–1939) seems to have had only a small influence on the rate of larceny as compared with the dramatic rise in burglary and robbery.

Larceny, of course, usually is a theft by stealth or cunning. Faced with the difficulties of tracking down thieves who left few clues, the Boston police may have been less successful in their detective work after the city reached a certain size. Also the major larceny of car theft was reported as a separate category after 1927 and Ferdinand did not take account of it in his comparisons. In other words, it is possible that the actual number of larcenies may still be rising, even though the rate of arrests seems to be falling.

INTERPRETING THE CRIME PATTERNS

Apparently, specific and unusual events, such as war or depression, have a fleeting but very powerful effect on the criminal behavior of a city's people. On the other hand, more subtle and gradual changes in the city's social class structure or way of life may also affect the crime rate. These long-term changes often occur so slowly that no difference can be seen from year to year. Only a long look backward can determine if there has been a general trend in any direction.

The economic cycle, with its constant ups and downs, has the most profound and recognizable effect on criminal behavior. Robberies, burglaries, and to some extent larcenies and assaults generally seem to rise during hard times. Major wars, too, seem to influence crime, since rape, burglary, assault, and larceny all tend to drop off during periods of armed conflict. Only murder and manslaughter seem totally unaffected by the influence of either warfare or economics.

At the same time—and quite independent of major national events—changes in the social structure of the local community also influence the criminal habits of its citizens. For example, the automobile apparently caused a rise in Boston's manslaughter rate and may also have played a role in pushing up the number of rapes.

More important is the growth of the city. As Boston grew in size, it lost many of the old small-town controls over its individual citizens. The big-city dweller had more freedom and independence. At the same time, he had fewer personal ties with other people in the city. Naturally, a freer and easier atmosphere is more favorable to crime. Surrounded by strangers rather than friends or relatives who might identify him, the criminal can operate with much less fear of detection or arrest.

There is also the fact that as Boston grew in size, it developed a well-organized underworld. This underworld not only sponsored a wide variety of crimes, but also provided a haven and a hiding place for criminals.

These developments tended to boost the crime rate. However, two other circumstances associated with the growth of the city were working simultaneously to push the crime rate down.

First, Boston was flooded by successive waves of immigrants from Ireland, Italy, and Eastern Europe. Although much has been written about "crooked Irish politicians" or "Mafia gangsters," the majority of the new arrivals were simply poor, hardworking peasants who wanted nothing more than a decent living. Indeed, the addition of so many honest, law-abiding, and industrious new citizens to the population actually lowered the overall crime rate by reducing the percentage of criminals.

Also, Boston's standard of living rose steadily throughout the period between 1849 and 1951, and the social structure of the city became reorganized and stabilized. In short, people stopped wandering and settled down, jobs got better and more plentiful, local industry prospered and expanded, and the immigrants became middle-class members of the community. The result, of course, was a decline in those crimes usually associated with economic hardship and social disorganization.

In the end, the increased number of honest citizens and the increased material comfort of life proved to be the strongest influences controlling and curtailing the crime rate—or, at least, until 1951.

CRIME SINCE 1951

Unfortunately, the statistical evidence of a declining crime rate is not confirmed by the more recent reports issued by the FBI and other law enforcement agencies. The recent rate in Boston is not going down—it is soaring skyward. This is made clear by the police statistics of 1967, sixteen years after Ferdinand's early study was completed. Although changes in the mode of reporting crimes made it impossible for him to produce a table which would correspond exactly with the data of his original study, the calculations do reveal a quite unmistakable trend in five of the major crimes.

NUMBER OF CRIMES PER 100,000 OF POPULATION

	1951	1967
Total Crime Rate .	179	 386
Murder and		
Manslaughter .	7	 12
Forcible Rape . .	9	 17
Robbery . . .	30	 80
Aggravated		
Assault . . .	28	 123
Burglary . . .	123	 154

Not only has the total crime rate very nearly doubled but the rate of each of these major crimes has risen substantially. But 16 years is a short time in the life of an old city. Ferdinand concludes that, broadly speaking, the current increase in urban violence and disorder still has not offset the general downward trend of crime since pre-Civil War days. Yet there is something ominous and disturbing about the new pattern.

For example, the rates of robbery and burglary have risen in the 1950s and 1960s, the most prosperous years in American history. Today's Bostonians are among the richest and most comfortable people who have ever lived. But these crimes usually increased so sharply only during times of depression. How, then, can those rising theft rates be explained?

One explanation may be found in the changing social character of Boston during the past two decades. Like many other big cities, Boston has lost large portions of its central city population to the suburbs. While Greater Boston has grown from two and one-half million to three and one-half million people since 1950, the old core city has dropped by almost 200,000 people. And, while it is less true of Boston than of many other cities, much of that lost population has been white and middle class.

While the children and grandchildren of Boston's immigrants flee to the suburbs, they leave behind in the inner city the unemployed and the uneducated, the ill-fed and the ill-housed. To these, many of whom belong to racial or ethnic minorities with limited opportunities, the affluent years of the 50s, 60s, and beyond are still hard times.

Although the rest of the nation may be enjoying prosperity, large segments of the urban population know only poverty and hardship. Thus, the growing theft and crime rates for the cities may really be responses to a *specialized* and *localized* kind of depression.

In addition, the slums, or lower-class neighborhoods, traditionally have been areas of the city with the highest crime rates. Indeed, in a great proportion of the crimes in the city, slum dwellers are the victims. If more and more of the city should turn into slum neighborhoods, the overall crime rate naturally might be expected to rise.

Paradoxically, our cities may not be dying because of rising crime rates. Instead, the opposite might be true: crime rates are rising because the cities are dying. Just as the downward trend of urban crime after the Civil War was associated with the growth of the cities into industrial, educational, and cultural centers, the new upward trend in crime may be associated with their decay.

Crime and Newcomers
to the City*

What are some of the new problems in daily life experienced by an individual who leaves the country to live in the city?

What differences are there between the norms of rural life and those of life in the slums of the cities?

How are these two sets of norms contradictory?

How may the changed conditions of the migrants' life show themselves in crime statistics as the Puerto Ricans become city people?

Sociologists studying the development of urban problems in Puerto Rico often have the feeling they are watching a rerun of a story about cities in the United States. It is as if they were seeing before their eyes a dramatization of parts of the history of the United States in the later part of the 19th century and the first years of the 20th century.

The Caribbean island of Puerto Rico, once a colony of the great Spanish Empire, came under the control of the United States after the Spanish-American War of 1898. Although the island has been within the United States' sphere of influence for nearly three-quarters of a century, it just recently began to be "modernized," or, more precisely, "Americanized."

Today, Puerto Rico has reached about the same stage of development as the United States had reached in the years immediately before and after the First World War, roughly from 1910 to 1920. The entire island is now experiencing rapid and dramatic social change, characterized by industrialization, im-

---

* Adapted from "Urbanization, Urbanism, and Deviant Behavior in Puerto Rico" by Marshall B. Clinard, *Social Change and Public Policy*, A Seminar at the University of Puerto Rico, 20–24 February 1967, Dr. Millard Hansen, ed. (Río Piedras: Social Science Research Center, University of Puerto Rico, 1968), pp. 24–36. Reprinted by permission.

proved standards of living, and increased educational opportunities.

This rapid modernization is not without its problems, however. The great economic advances have not meant happiness for all the people, nor have they solved old social problems. On the contrary: the modernization of Puerto Rico is creating new and more serious difficulties.

URBANIZATION AND CRIME

The most extensive and obvious social change in Puerto Rico has been urbanization—the move of people in great numbers from farms to cities. Once a simple farming country, Puerto Rico is now nearly a society of city-dwellers, with more than 50 percent of its population living in urban areas. Metropolitan San Juan, for example, now has a population of at least 700,000, or approximately one in four of the Puerto Ricans, but in 1960 the city itself numbered only 451,658. The smaller market towns of Ponce and Mayaguez have become fair-sized cities. And the entire island seems to reflect new urban tastes and interests. Newspapers and radio reach every home, the islanders travel back and forth between mainland cities and island farms, and the tourists bring modern facilities into even remote corners.

Urbanization is probably Puerto Rico's greatest social change and undoubtedly the rising crime rate is the most serious consequence of the change. Juvenile delinquency, for example, increased by five to six times in just the years between 1956 and 1964, when a total of 2,542 arrests jumped to a total of 12,768. Other more serious crimes have increased even more. Drug addiction was virtually unknown in the 1950s, but the Island had more than 11,000 addicts, most of them youthful, by 1966.

The close connection between urbanization and crime is no coincidence, nor is it unique to Puerto Rico. Indeed, Professor Marshall B. Clinard of the University of Wisconsin has watched the same patterns of change and problems produced by urban development in the United States and in Sweden. He has watched the pattern being repeated in the Caribbean Island of Puerto Rico and what follows is an interpretation of his comment on the relationship between city life and crime.

Something about city life sets the urban dweller apart from his rural counterparts. Like other sociologists, Clinard argues that it is the freedom of city life. Released from the restraints and restrictions of the small town or village, the new arrival in the city finds he can do almost anything he likes—or thinks he can. While this freedom may encourage productive and creative activity, it also lays him open to the temptation to engage in delinquency and crime. In an atmosphere of greater temptations and fewer controls, the rates of crime, prostitution, alcoholism, and suicide naturally rise.

Of course, the typical migrant from the farm does not move to the city with a conscious desire to cause trouble or to lose himself in worldly pleasures. Nor is he mentally disturbed, criminally inclined, or morally weak. Most migrants are solid, sincere, citizens who want only to make a better life for themselves and their families. Unfortunately, many of them are simply overwhelmed by the sudden startling cultural shock of city life.

Consider what a terrifying thing the city must be for a simple, uneducated man such as Juan García. Juan has lived on a Puerto Rican farm all his life and has never before been away from his small village. Suddenly, within hours after his arrival in a strange city, he must: 1) find a new and completely unfamiliar way of making a living; 2) work at regular "city" hours; 3) go without the advice and help of his family; 4) cope with the pushing, shoving mobs of strangers; 5) find new ways of communicating, traveling, dressing, eating, and even relaxing; and 6) become used to working, sleeping, eating, and living in the dirt, noise, crowding, and confusion of the city.

On top of all these immediate problems, Juan must make some more serious adjustments. For years, he has lived on a "subsistence economy," that is, he raised all his own food, milked his own cows, sewed his own clothes (or his wife did), and perhaps earned a few dollars selling vegetables he grew himself, to pay for other necessities. He did not expect to produce more than just enough goods and food for his own family. Moreover, his life was tied to an agricultural cycle, working frantically at planting and harvest time and doing very little all the rest of the year.

In the city, however, Juan discovers that everything is bought in cold, hard cash—there is no bartering, no exchange, no raising of your own food. Worse yet, life in the city is not dependent on planting and harvesting. This urban society constantly demands money and a man must have a full-time job to survive. Or he must find some other ways to make money.

Back home, Juan at least had his family and friends to give him courage, help, and advice in times of trouble. Here in the city, he does not know where to turn for help. Most city agencies are mysterious, forbidding bureaucracies that know nothing about him. The lines of communication between Juan and the specialists—social workers, vocational counsellors, and others—who might aid him are clogged with red tape, official forms, and special regulations. Juan and thousands of migrants like him become more and more bewildered by the city.

Juan's bewilderment may eventually turn to bitterness and dislike of the city—and its representatives. The city seems to ignore him. Because he cannot understand the restrictions and regulations there, he pays little attention to them.

As with most migrants looking for cheap housing, he comes to reside in one of the many slum communities in San Juan. Here the way of life is characterized not only by poor sanitation and health practices but by norms favoring a high incidence of delinquency, crime, prostitution, drug addiction, and alcoholism. Stolen goods are frequently for sale there. There are many gangs of young males in the slums who engage in stealing. Juan makes friends with members of one of these groups and learns techniques of stealing as well as rationalizations to excuse it.

Back where Juan came from, the tight little community set standards of behavior for all the members of the village. In the big, impersonal city, the controls over behavior are the official rules of the police and welfare departments and the opinions of the neighbors, if he knows them well enough to care. But Juan soon learns that police officers or welfare workers are not always on hand to enforce the rules. Besides, the law is not the same for everyone: some who break the law go free. More important, breaking the formal rules in the city does not mean Juan will be condemned as he might be for breaking with the unwritten traditions of home. In fact, if Juan can break the law often enough without getting caught, he may gain fame and admiration as a "smart guy" or a "wheeler and dealer."

In this difficult, puzzling situation, a migrant like Juan eventually becomes more adjusted to the ways and norms of city life and the slums. And because of this change that takes place among migrants, crime rates rise drastically as a country becomes urbanized.

SLUMS AND PUBLIC HOUSING

Although the problems of urban adjustment and the rising rates of crime are widespread throughout Puerto Rico, a disproportionate amount of crime is concentrated in the slums and housing projects in and around San Juan and other big cities. This is true, too, of the mainland.

According to the 1967 Report of the President's Commission on Law Enforcement, "the most serious crimes that worry people most—murder, forcible rape, aggravated assault, burglary—happen most often in the slums of large cities. . . . The *offenses*, the *victims*, and the *offenders* are found most frequently in the poorest and most deteriorated and socially disorganized areas of the cities."

Not only do many crimes occur in the slums, but a great proportion of crime is committed against slum dwellers. Most fights, robberies, and assaults occur on slum streets and involve people who live in these neighborhoods. The victims of rape are almost always from the slums. The slum adolescents who use drugs complicate the lives of their own families and friends, not the lives of people living elsewhere. And the public problems of sanitation and health most directly affect the slum dwellers, not the people in more prosperous and protected neighborhoods.

In Puerto Rico, too, those people who commit crimes are usually residents of either the slums or the housing projects in slum clearance areas. A recent study shows that the rates of arrests of San Juan delinquents are highest in the Slum Belt (1.7 per 1000 population), Old City (1.6), and Central District (1.2), while the Beach Front tourist area has a rate of only 0.4.

By contrast with other cities, however, the rate at which delinquent acts are committed is almost in the reverse order, with the greatest number of crimes committed in the Beach Front area. This implies that delinquent acts in San Juan are often committed by individuals or gangs raiding the more prosperous neighborhoods. Naturally, this only adds to the fear of middle-class residents. It may partly explain their flight to the suburbs.

As slum dwellers become more and more feared and isolated from the rest of the city, they, in turn, grow suspicious and hostile. The people of the slums develop their own way of life* and their standards and values are almost completely the opposite of the official standards set down by the city government. But every city agency needs local "grass roots" cooperation if conditions of a neighborhood are to be improved. Obviously, the police cannot wipe out gambling and fighting if such activities are approved and admired—as they were back in Juan's village, where men gambled for a pastime and fought to prove their manly strength. Prostitution is an offense in the eyes of the authorities but it may be accepted in the slum as one way in which a woman living in poverty and without marketable skills can lay her hands on the ready cash which is always needed when one lives in a city.

The physical condition of a neighborhood is not the only measure of a slum. Another measure is the slum way of life. Its behavior patterns often persist even after the slums are gone (as in slum clearance projects) or the people have moved away. And sometimes they appear in parts of the city which are not really slums at all. An instance is the public housing projects in Puerto Rico, known as caseríos. The caseríos are not physically slums. In fact, most have adequate facilities and are quite modern and attractive. Yet the rates of delinquency and crime are high there.

Surveys show that the residents of these housing projects generally dislike both the social conditions and the official regulations which go with living in caseríos.

For one thing, many of the rules of the caseríos are contrary to the accepted standards of the rural life from which the people of the caseríos came. They object, for instance, to the rule against great numbers of people crowding into the same dwelling. Juan would never turn away a relative. But he would find it easy to break a city ordinance by sharing his room with a kinsman or close friend. If he lived in a caserío, Juan would also complain of

* See "Lower-Class Culture and Delinquency" in this book.

the financial restrictions, rules of sanitation, and a host of other minor irritations. The surveys reveal that inhabitants of public housing dislike both their homes and their neighbors. Only 7 percent of the fathers said a caserío is a good place to rear children.

The slums in Puerto Rico have grown up, haphazardly and bit by bit, often as a result of squatters who establish themselves on land too swampy to support commercial buildings or on hillsides too steep for other uses. They are overcrowded, smelly, noisy, dirty, unhealthy, and generally condemned by the rest of the city. Still, the slum's inhabitants are fonder of their home than the caserío-dwellers are of their new apartment houses. And the unpopularity of the new housing seems due to the lack of any sense of the community, the lack of personal freedom, and the overpowering presence of the impersonal management of the buildings. Caseríos, in short, offer the very opposite of the warm, intimate life of the village, and in this respect the public housing projects and the slums are much alike. Unfortunately they resemble each other in precisely the circumstances that make for high rates of delinquency and crime. And they offer clear evidence that merely wiping out the slums would not do away with unlawful behavior.

It is not simple poverty which explains why the caseríos and the slums are the breeding grounds of crime. It is the historic process played out in the 18th and 19th centuries and on into the 20th century in Western Europe and the United States. The man from the village or the farm suffers from a loss of community support and of the personal sense of identification with the community when he moves to the city, and he feels free to engage in behavior he would have avoided at home.* When he and others like him move, they add to the population of the city, and in the impersonal conditions of life they find there they may turn from law-abiding to lawbreaking.

* See "Urbanism as a Way of Life" in *Cities and City Life* in this *Readings in Sociology* Series.

Organized Crime and
Its Social Effects*

What does it mean to call certain offenses "organized crimes"?

How is organized crime different from other crime?

Is organized crime like a business enterprise? In what ways do organized crime and business enterprises **not** resemble each other?

What are some of the effects on the community itself, of organized crime?

Why is it so difficult to suppress organized crime?

The stolen-car racket in New York City is so well managed that anyone who risks buying a car from it can give his specifications—make of car, model, even color of body—at 9 A.M., and, it is said, the car he ordered will be delivered to him by noon. This is less time than most honest car agencies need for filling an order. How is it done?

Early in December, 1968, three former employees of the Department of Motor Vehicles of the State of New York together with 27 others were arrested and charged with being members of a "hot" (stolen) car "ring," operating in several states. With their arrest the District Attorney of the Borough of Queens (a part of metropolitan New York City) revealed a very big business, for the "ring" or "racket" arranged the thefts and sale of over one thousand cars a year, specializing in recent models of Cadillacs.

An operation of this size requires organization and business ability such as are needed for the profitable running of a legiti-

* Adapted from "Organized Crime: Challenge to the American Legal System" by Earl Johnson, Jr., *Journal of Criminal Law, Criminology, and Police Science,* Vol. 53, No. 4 (December 1962), pp. 399–425. Reprinted by permission.

mate automobile sales agency. But these are stolen cars, and big business in stolen cars means *big* crime. And it means wide-scale corruption, as well. This New York ring had been in existence for ten years.

The ring's method of operating is this: "spotters" are paid to make lists of cars that could be stolen on short notice. The men who are hired to do the actual stealing take the stolen cars to mechanics who change engine numbers in the ring's repair shops and make other changes so that the stolen car will suit the requirements of the customer. They may, for example, change the color of the car or screw on a particular type of side-view mirror. A late model stolen Cadillac might be sold for as little as $1800. The ring keeps a few cars in storage at all times and thus is able to fill some orders immediately. But more often a car to match what the customer wants is picked from the spotters' lists and stolen "to order."

Before the car is delivered to the customer, the proper papers must be provided to go with it, giving evidence of the sale and new ownership. Here forgers are needed. And two women clerks in the office of the Registry of Motor Vehicles and, with them, a man employed there as a guard were found to be on the ring's extensive payroll. They made out false registration papers, sales stubs, proof of insurance, and any other documents which would make the deal look honest and "prove" that the ring's customer was the "true" owner of the car. Each of these three state employees received $150 from the ring for every stolen car he helped to register.

The operations of this large criminal enterprise came to light in the course of the investigation by the police of the murder of a Mafia racketeer who was reported to be the mastermind behind the ring.

How much crime is involved in this large illegal operation?

First, there are the spotters, who are accomplices of the men who steal the cars. The mechanics are also "parties," to use the legal term, to the theft. And, of course, there is the "sales staff," the employees of the ring who take orders from the customers and those who deliver the car to the new "owner" and complete the deal. And there is the customer who knows full well that if he is sold a nearly new Cadillac for, it may be, a tenth of its normal price, it is not an honest transaction. He, too, breaks the law, for he is the "receiver of stolen goods." And there is the murder, inspired, no doubt, by some associate of the dead man who craved a larger share of the power and the money.

Aside from the murder, perhaps the worst crime is that of the clerks and the guard in the office where vehicles are registered with the State of New York. For this is not simple theft: it is bribery and corruption and a betrayal of public trust. These three offenders may make less money than any of the others who are involved, but they are robbing all the citizens of the state, as well as the rightful owner of the stolen car.

The "ring," the "racket," the "syndicate," the "gang" are the common names for criminal business organizations. But for the fact that they make their profits by breaking the law, they are, at least in form, very like honest business organizations. Indeed, they are more like legitimate commercial undertakings than they arc like other criminal enterprises because they expect to keep on indefinitely. Burglars may "bring off a job" in pairs, or three people may plan a murder, but once the deed is done they usu ally do not look forward to years of operating together. Organized crime goes on and on and often gets bigger and bigger.

As a Special Attorney in the Organized Crime and Racketeering Section of the United States Department of Justice, Dr. Earl Johnson, Jr., evaluated the threat to American society which lies in organized crime. He probed into organized crime's extent and its seemingly invincible power. The pages which follow tell about his analysis.

The name "Mafia" refers to a perfect example of a criminal organization. Beginning as an association of certain families in Sicily who preyed upon their neighbors and took the law into their own hands, avenging murder with murder, the Mafia was extended to the United States by Italian immigrants and is now a huge organization, operating on both the European and North American continents. Today the term "Mafia" is quite commonly applied to certain criminal organizations whose membership is not confined to Italians.

The money which these "brotherhoods of evil" extract from society can never be exactly stated, for, naturally, those who know the facts keep them secret. It is estimated by the Department of Justice to run into billions of dollars. Six fields of endeavor appear to be especially profitable to criminal organizations at present: (1) illegal gambling, which has been estimated to bring in at least $20 billion a year, (2) the narcotics traffic, which probably yields the highest rate of return,* (3) racketeering, or the extortion of money from legitimate enterprises, (4) prostitution, which is still a large business, though shrinking, (5) "shylocking," a new, widespread enterprise in loaning money at exorbitant rates of interest, and (6) legitimate businesses.

The last named is a field of operation new to the criminal syndicates and one which is gaining rapidly in importance. In many cities, criminals dominate the distribution of juke boxes and vending machines. Laundry services, the retailing of beer and liquor, the ownership of nightclubs, food wholesaling, record manufacturing, and garment-making are other businesses in which gangs also have substantial stakes. When a criminal organization enters any of these or similar commercial enterprises, it uses force and fear to secure a monopoly, and when it has finally succeeded in driving competitors out of business, it raises prices to exorbitant levels. Thus it not only robs the public of millions but also entices customers from legitimate, law-abiding firms and ultimately forces many to close their doors.

The economic cost of organized crime is more than matched by the human cost. Although the number of gangland killings has decreased considerably from the heydey of Al Capone in Chicago in the 1920s, organized crime is still responsible for more murders than any other element of equal size in the population of the United States. And an increasing proportion of the victims today are ordinary citizens who refused to yield when threatened by the syndicate or who dared to appear in court against it, or who refused to pay the interest rates it demands. In Chicago, for example, Joseph Bronge, a beer distributor, was killed when he refused to make deals with a gangster who had gained control

* See "Cats, Kicks, and Color" in *Cities and City Life* in this *Readings in Sociology* Series, also "Drugs and Drug Users" in this book.

over the sale of a popular brand of beer. And, John Arthur Powers was ambushed and shot five times shortly after he confided to a friend that he owed the "Outfit" $1800.

The physical toll taken by organized crime, however, is not limited to murder. A great many more people are simply beaten or maimed, on the sound theory that a terrified adversary is virtually as good as a dead one. And, beyond all this, thousands of accidental natural deaths and illnesses are traceable to the narcotics which the narcotics rings distribute.

The most frightening thing about organized crime is that it is never satisfied: it always wants more. This leads it to the steadily increasing exploitation of human weaknesses.

In the first place, one of the effects of syndicate operations is the steady expansion of vice. Organized crime is often defended on the ground that its activities in the worlds of gambling, prostitution, and narcotics merely satisfy the wants and wishes of certain of the populace. In actual fact, however, organized crime consciously and systematically strives to encourage and cultivate these appetites in order to grow rich through catering to them.

This is particularly true in the matter of narcotics and other drugs. It is not coincidence that the men who illicitly retail narcotics are called "pushers." Their efforts are concentrated on "hooking" the most susceptible and innocent element in the population—the teen-agers. Many addicts can trace their lifelong miseries to a free marijuana cigarette offered by a "friendly stranger" in the schoolyard and puffed secretly during recess.

Secondly, the groups give encouragement to people on the outside to engage in criminal behavior. Many of the illegal products and services marketed by criminal organizations carry with them a dangerous by-product of crime—crime committed not by the rings or rackets themselves but by their customers. For example, the teller of a suburban bank outside Chicago was jailed for embezzling almost $45,000 from his employer in order to gamble on the horse races. Less than a fortnight after this, a second Chicago teller, who also had been betting, was arrested for embezzling $2000—in a fruitless effort to "beat a neighborhood book."

More numerous are the crimes committed by men and women and boys and girls who are lured into the habit of taking drugs. For it may cost an addict $50 a day to pay for the supply of drugs he (or she) needs, once he is "hooked." Since narcotics are banned by law, drug peddlers can demand outrageous prices. As a result, a teen-ager who has always been honest may end up rifling empty apartments and snatching handbags to get the cash he needs to pay for his habit.

A few athletes are corrupted by gangland. Of the billions wagered by the public in the gambling outlets of organized crime, the biggest percentage is risked on the outcome of athletic contests. But even though the betting pools are arranged so as to give the operators a dependable and handsome profit, greedy criminals are never content. Hence their efforts to bribe key athletes to play badly in games where most betters expect them to win.

People who oppose gambling of any kind may argue that the betters who are defrauded in this way are getting their "just desserts." But no one should overlook the fact that tampering with athletic events injures nonbetting enthusiasts by destroying their interest in the corrupted sports. Consider, for instance, what has happened to boxing. Once it was a sport enjoyed by millions of Americans, but fixed bouts have given it such a bad reputation that it is now of interest to only a tiny minority.

In the third place, the gangs attack the very institutions on which free society is founded. In order to shield its antisocial activities, organized crime works hard to capture or, at least, to render ineffective those who are charged with enforcing the law. At various times, criminal organizations have been powerful political forces in New York, Chicago, Detroit, Philadelphia, Miami, and New Orleans. And in many smaller communities they have virtually reigned supreme. Even high-ranking state officials have occasionally been allied with organized crime. New Jersey, for instance, was rocked in 1959 and again in 1969 by investigations revealing sinister connections between a number of state leaders and the local members of the Mafia.

It is obvious that proper service cannot be rendered to the people by those politicians, bureaucrats, legislators, police officers, prosecutors, and judges who owe allegiance to organized crime. They not only accede to the gang's direct requests even when these run counter to the public's interests, but, perhaps worse than that, they reach such a state of mixed terror and loyalty that, in whatever they do, they wonder and worry about how the gang may be affected. And, once they become accustomed to accepting bribes and rewards from criminals, they begin to expect payments on the side from everyone else and for everything they do.

In fiction, crooked politicians are often depicted as smart. But the truth is that the men and women who are attracted to playing corrupt parts in the government are usually of inferior ability. Thus the public is "short-changed" even when the officials are acting honestly.

The public is also ill served when organized crime seeks to insure victory to its candidates for election by threatening and bribing voters, "stuffing" ballot boxes, and causing miscounts of the votes. This not only brings into office dishonest and incompetent people but also defrauds the honest voter of his right to cast a vote which carries the same weight as every other man's vote.

Finally, in the long run, society's basic moral standards are undermined by the thieving and graft of criminal organizations. Unlike burglars, con men, and other criminals who ply their trade in secret, making every effort to avoid being detected, organized crime operates in the open but protects itself by buying immunity from indictment and prosecution. Consequently, whereas successful burglars have very little impact on the morale and morality of the law-abiding public because they are not visible, organized crime, by its very openness and publicity, advertises how profitable evil may be. This undoubtedly encourages the foolish, the weak, and the desperate to engage in criminal activities.* It encourages many others, too, to make questionable compromises with the accepted legal and moral codes. A man with the gang's money to spend can easily corrupt the boys in a corner gang: by doing them favors he can enlist them as minor helpers in gang activities, from which they may graduate in time into real gang membership.

* See "The Candidate for Delinquency" and "The Slum: Opportunities for Crime and Delinquency" in this book.

The indifference to organized crime which prevails in most places is the product of many circumstances. In the first place, the bulk of the income of criminal organizations is not derived from activities which deprive people of their property by force or deceit. Rather, it is obtained from enterprises, such as gambling, which provide people with commodities or services they *want*. Accordingly, organized crime ordinarily does not make indignant, vengeful victims in the same way that everyday burglars and muggers do. Furthermore, gangsters are, as a rule, not bothered by the public. Except for the narcotics traffic, most gangland activities are not considered sufficiently immoral to cause the majority of Americans to take an active stand against them. That is why it has been possible for criminals to organize and make a safe place for themselves year after year.

Graft, Gambling, and
Public Opinion*

American laws often condemn behavior which is ignored or tolerated in other societies. Are these criminal laws really supported by
the people?

Can city police departments count upon the support of the people
in enforcing the laws?

How does organized crime get a foothold in local politics? How
does local corruption work? What do the people think about it?

Wincanton certainly is not a tourist attraction. The city has
little natural charm and absolutely no man-made beauty. The
major highways crossing the state do their best to avoid Wincanton. If a traveler is unfortunate enough to get off the turnpike
and on to the truck route, he sees only Wincanton's grimy slums
and warehouse sections.

The 100,000 people of Wincanton are an uneven mix of
Germans, Irish, Italians, Poles, and blacks—in that order of numbers and prosperity.

Wincanton was once a thriving mill town which supplied
nearly a tenth of the nation's knitted goods. But the mill owners
moved south to find cheaper labor and lower taxes, leaving their
gloomy brick mills behind as monuments to Wincanton's past
fame. Today these buildings have been broken up into scores of
tiny factories within factories which manufacture everything
from ball-point pens to zippers.

Wincanton does not have any single major industry. Unless,
of course, it is *organized crime*, which before 1964 might have
been described as an industry.

* Adapted from "Public Attitudes Toward Gambling and Corruption" by
John A. Gardiner, *Annals of the American Academy of Political and Social
Science*, Vol. 374 (November 1967), pp. 123–134. Reprinted by permission.

Crime was in those days a big business in Wincanton. For most of the past 40 years, Wincanton has been "wide open." The local officials had protected the numbers rackets, prostitution, race-track betting, and gambling operations for high stakes, run by "the syndicate." In addition, the politicians engaged in their own free-lance corruption—extorting "kickbacks" from the city's sales and purchases, from the granting of city licenses, from the fixing of legal cases, and from almost anything else that men in power can do for a price.

Naturally, Wincanton's reputation was well known. The city served as a regional center for the syndicate in that part of the state. Crime bosses from other nearby cities regularly held conferences in Wincanton. Out-of-town gamblers arrived daily for major dice games. Even students from neighboring colleges visited town to sample its illegal pastimes.

Yet, only three times between the end of World War II and 1968 did Wincanton voters reject politicians linked with racketeers. Only three times had the people actively endorsed and supported reform candidates who promised to "clean up the city." Significantly, each of these reform movements immediately followed some major federal investigation which brought unfavorable national publicity to the city.

Graft, corruption, and other forms of cheating the public by public officials can exist only if the public tolerates them. If a public servant pockets money paid to the city for licenses to engage in retail business, and other officials know but do not object to it, then they are to be regarded as consenting to the crime. By looking on while the city is being robbed, the other public servants share the guilt of those who actually take the money. Some kinds of grafters and racketeers are very commonly tolerated. Others are indignantly denounced.

John Gardiner, a political scientist at the State University of New York at Stony Brook, sought to find out what attitudes people take toward two kinds of large-scale lawbreaking— graft and gambling. He used as his laboratory the residents of Wincanton.

Judged only by their voting record, the people of Wincanton seemed generally unconcerned about gambling and other types of nonviolent crime. The Wincantonites appeared, too, to be only moderately well informed about either local law-enforcement processes or politics. And, finally, they grew highly indignant and moralistic about official wrongdoing when it brought shame on the city.

To understand better why crises were necessary to shake up the people of Wincanton, Professor Gardiner brought a team of interviewers to the city during one of its rare "reform periods." They asked questions about the public's attitude toward gambling, corruption, and politics. The opinions of Wincantonites perhaps help explain the long and highly successful life of organized crime in their city and in other parts of the United States.

"People will always gamble. . . ." The primary and almost indispensable financial base of any crime syndicate is gambling. Every two-dollar bet placed in a bookie joint goes into the syndicate's treasury, where it may be used to finance loan shark operations, or drug traffic, or other unlawful businesses. That two dollars also helps pay the expenses of buying off politicians and public employees. The profits go to the crime bosses and the public pays the final price through higher taxes.

The Wincanton crime syndicate was headed by Irv Stern, a resident of the city. Under Irv's expert direction, the syndicate provided Wincantonites with numbers rackets, off-track betting, sports pools, lotteries, and dice games for high stakes. From time to time—depending on the vigilance of Federal authorities— slot machines and pinball machines of the type that pay off were also openly installed in bars and restaurants.

In addition, taking advantage of Irv's organized and illegal activities, Wincantonites enjoyed other, legalized forms of gambling: "Las Vegas nights" sponsored by churches, Boy Scout raffles, slot machines in private clubs, and bingo games operated nightly, largely for the entertainment of elderly women. These were the conditions up to 1964.

In 1966, two years after a new "reform" mayor had closed down—or at least driven underground—all the illegal gambling operations and bingo had been outlawed by the state, the people of Wincanton were asked their opinions about gambling. They were remarkably tolerant.

Almost everyone (96 percent) agreed that "No matter what you do, people will always gamble." Gambling, they thought, was simply a fact of life. Most Wincantonites admitted gambling and liking it. And they suspected that their neighbors did, too.

Besides believing that gambling was widespread throughout the community, many Wincantonites felt that certain kinds of gambling were perfectly all right. For example, 88 percent felt that churches and other charitable organizations should be allowed to hold bingo games. Nearly 60 percent thought the state should legalize *all* gambling and even run its own lottery to support the public schools. Getting closer home, about half of the people interviewed felt the police "should not break up a friendly poker game, even if betting was going on."

"This is a case for the Federal authorities. . . ." Obviously, the residents of Wincanton felt quite at ease with gambling. They certainly were not shocked by it. On the other hand, Wincantonites seemed to know—or care—relatively little about the law-enforcement processes in their hometown.

Although 90 percent of the people interviewed could name the mayor and 63 percent knew the name of their Congressman, only 36 percent recognized the name of the present district attorney. (Ironically, 55 percent could name his predecessor, a much more flamboyant but much less effective official.)

Knowledge or even mere awareness of any reforms undertaken by the district attorney's office was also skimpy. More than half of the people had no idea at all whether the office had changed its crime-suppressing activities since the last administration.

When asked "which Federal agency was responsible for most local arrests and prosecutions of Wincanton people during the past ten years," about a third correctly identified the Internal Revenue Service as the busiest law enforcement agency. But 20 percent said it was the FBI; but the FBI had conducted only *one* gambling raid in a decade. Forty-six percent of the people simply did not know.

Strangely enough, most Wincantonites knew little about the details or techniques of "gang-busting," but nearly 60 percent thought the reform-minded mayor was doing a good job. And many people specifically mentioned "better law enforcement" and "less corruption" as reasons.

Ironically, too, people generally defended the mayor's "crackdown" on gambling, despite their stated desire to have more of it. In fact, 67 percent of the people even thought the bingo parlors should remain closed as long as the law made the game illegal.

"Give us good, clean government. . . ." Obviously, there are some serious contradictions in the typical Wincantonite's public attitude toward crime and corruption. He wants to enjoy the pleasures of gambling, but he also wants his elected officials to enforce the laws which make gambling illegal. He will tolerate gambling in his city, but not the dishonesty and double-dealing by politicians which can make gambling possible. In fact, interviews with Wincantonites reveal that they set rather high standards for their officials—at least high when compared with their standards as to gambling.

For example, 73 percent disagreed with the statement: "A city official should not be punished for receiving $10 in cash from a company which does business with the city." Sixty-three percent of the people also disagreed with the statement: "It's all right for the mayor to make a profit when the city buys land as long as the city gets a fair price." And more than half of the people even disapproved of the mayor or police "fixing speeding tickets."

The general disapproval of corruption fell to only 47 percent, however, when the statements were restated as: "City officials can accept presents as long as taxpayers do not suffer." Perhaps this more easygoing attitude indicates that the public naturally expects at least a *little* corruption in high places.

"I didn't know it existed. . . ." If Wincantonites generally want dependable and honest elected officials, how can they ignore the evidence that organized crime is corrupting City Hall? The laws against prostitution, gambling, and narcotics traffic are so clear-cut and tough that for them to exist unchecked, somebody on the public payroll who should be a watchdog of the people's interests must be looking the other way. Yet

most people do not see the connection between official corruption and organized crime. Why do they not see this connection?

One reason may be the relatively low visibility of corruption in Wincanton—or any city. Wincanton's big gambling operation—the "floating crap game"—was well hidden at various locations in the city, and it usually catered only to out-of-towners. The newspapers said very little about this form of gambling, and few people realized it existed until the FBI one night finally broke in upon the game.

By contrast, the pinball machines, the bookie shops, and the numbers rackets must have been visible to everyone. These are forms of gambling on a massive scale which depend on large numbers of people placing bets in cigar stores, passing policy slips on street corners, and playing pinball in bars and restaurants. Of course, the average man seldom realizes that payoffs to politicians allow these activities to survive, unless someone—such as a newspaper or an investigating committee—calls it to his attention.

Official corruption is probably least visible when it involves the under-the-table wheeling and dealing of local politicians in "kickbacks," "rakeoffs," and "markups." Direct contacts with these shady deals at City Hall are usually limited to the officials and the businessmen involved.

Of course, if one explanation of the public's ignorance about official corruption is its invisibility, another is simply public *apathy*. Local affairs are generally of very little interest to the man in the street. Only 9 percent of the people in Wincanton reported being "extremely interested" in city politics, while 78 percent were only "moderately" or "not much" interested. In other words, almost anything could happen at City Hall and nobody would pay it much attention.

In addition to apathy, there is also the general feeling that "everyone is a little corrupt." For example, most Wincanton residents thought their new administration was "better than the last," but only a tiny 11 percent thought that *no* policemen or city councilman would ever take a bribe. Naturally, when people come to expect minor graft as normal, only large-scale corruption —"a $5 million land grab or a $60,000 kickback"—will ever stir them up.

"It couldn't happen here. . . ." But sometimes an apathetic public can be roused out of its indifference by influences from the outside, too.

Three times in recent history, Wincanton's voters have been stirred up enough to break their old voting habits and elect reform candidates. In each instance, the reform movement began as an answer to unfavorable nationwide publicity about the city.

In the early 1950s, a Congressional committee investigating organized crime singled out Wincanton as a "classic example of the political strangulation of a police department at the request of the gambling interests." Irv Stern's gambling activities were aired in Washington. Payoffs to patrolmen and city officials were uncovered and local politicians were nationally condemned.

Twelve years later, Wincanton suffered the same embarrassment when the United States Justice Department indicted the chief of police on perjury charges brought on by his testimony about the city's hiring of towing firms, and the mayor and Irv Stern on charges of extorting kickbacks when the city purchased parking meters.

Finally, two days before the primary elections of 1967, the National Crime Commission reported the city's apathy toward thirty years of gambling and corruption. The local newspaper ran the news in banner headlines: "U.S. CRIME COMMISSION PINPOINTS WINCANTON AND ITS APATHY."

Following each of these exposés, Wincanton voters did the unexpected. They voted out the offending politicians. Why this sudden change of heart? Why this complete disapproval of a system they had supported for so long?

According to those engaged in the study of Wincanton, the exposés created "crisis situations" which forced the public to realize the contradiction in their toleration of organized crime and their simultaneous demand for honesty in government. Outraged and embarrassed, the voters used the ballot box to restore their own sense of morality—and to brighten their tarnished image in the eyes of the outside world.

"Things must be different elsewhere. . . ." Many Americans seem to share the attitudes of Wincantonites. For example, most Americans seem much more tolerant of gambling than the laws

would have us believe. In other words, few people really consider gambling harmful or dangerous, yet gambling is either illegal or severely restricted in almost every state. There are, it seems, many people willing to ignore the law in order to "place a harmless little bet." Incidentally, gambling is a matter on which there are wide differences of opinion. Britain is said to have more facilities for gambling than any other country in the Western World. It has 1,000 casinos in contrast to 150 in France. But the state of Nevada has more casinos than there are in Britain.

Most Americans value honesty and good administration, but do not really expect officials to live up to their promises. Indeed, those people who like the special services of the crime syndicates probably hope that the law will bend a little.

And most Americans are not aware how deep the corruption runs in their cities. Even fewer people understand the close—and absolutely necessary—relationship between organized crime and crooked politicians.

Happily, Wincanton does seem to offer one slim promise of hope. In that city, the people became outraged when they were shown how gangsters controlled their politicians. Given a clear-cut, unqualified, and dramatic choice between honest government and crooked government, other Americans may grow angry enough to "throw the bums out."

Riots· Past and Present Violence*

Does the current violence in our country differ in quality or quantity from the violence of the past?

Why do cycles of violence occur in some historical periods but not in others?

If cycles of violence occur not because man is by nature violent but because of social causes, what is the nature of those social causes?

If we understand the social causes, can we use this understanding to prevent a recurrence of cycles of violence in the future?

Americans think of themselves as quiet, peace-loving, reasonable people. They believe their country is guided by democratic, rational, and peace-loving principles.

But is this conception true to the facts?

Actually, the United States always has been a violent country. Its history is marked by repeated cycles of violence and wide-scale rioting—which are always soon forgotten. Perhaps they are forgotten because no one wishes to remember them, for the examples of violence in the past do not fit well with the American self-image of a peaceful democracy.

THE CYCLE OF VIOLENCE

Americans have forgotten about Shays' Rebellion of 1786, for instance, when a group of impoverished farmers from western Massachusetts, angered by unfair state taxes, simply seized the

* Adapted from "Psychological Factors in Riots—Old and New" by John P. Spiegel, American Journal of Psychiatry, Vol. 125, No. 3 (September 1968), pp. 281–285. Copyright © 1968, the American Psychiatric Association. Reprinted by permission.

law courts and refused to let trials be conducted. This rebellion so frightened the state legislators that the tax laws were almost immediately modified.

Americans also have forgotten about the anti-Catholic (actually, anti-Irish) riots of the 1840s and 1850s. Forgotten, too, are the Civil War draft riots of 1863 when, in the city of New York alone, more than two thousand people were killed in five days. And so are the extraordinarily cruel anti-Chinese riots on the West Coast during the 1870s—to say nothing of the hideous lynching mobs which between 1890 and 1900 accounted for the brutal murders of 166 blacks a year and as late as 1927 for 38 a year. No one but an historian ever gives a thought to the anti-Negro riots of 1919–1920. More than 16,000 Federal troops were needed to quell rioting and destruction during the Pullman Strike of the 1890s. And Americans even have forgotten the bloody, brutal labor struggles at the turn of the century and during the Depression.

The current wave of rioting by students on college campuses and by blacks in urban communities is only another round in the cycle of violence which has racked the United States at least seven times since the Declaration of Independence.

This all too common aspect of American life has been studied by Dr. John P. Spiegel, who is the director of the Lemberg Center for the Study of Violence at Brandeis University. He and his staff have collected reports of riots and violent outbreaks in the past. To these they add detailed accounts of present-day episodes of violence, wherever they occur in the nation.

Dr. Spiegel began his research with the question: What is violence? The word is used by news commentators and popular writers to cover a multitude of sins and crimes; but for sociologists it has a very special meaning. Violence, as Dr. Spiegel defines it, is the extreme type at one end of a whole range of behavior called aggression. Aggression is behavior by which one individual compels another to do something against his will. Violence, therefore, is that very specialized form of aggression which includes the use of force directed against persons, objects, or organizations with the specific intent of injuring or destroying.

Of course, many kinds of violence are found in American life —from the insane violence of a lone assassin to the organized violence of a crime syndicate, and to the officially organized, formal violence of a nation at war. Perhaps the violence most observed—and least understood—today is the collective violence associated with urban disturbances, college sit-ins, and black rioting.

Collective violence is destructive physical aggression by a group which supports and encourages the violence of its individual members. Collective violence differs in part from other forms of aggression because of its explosiveness. The violence of the crowd is released suddenly and fully.

In today's American life, collective violence occurs in three principal forms: the violence of whites against blacks, the violence of blacks against whites, and the violence of police and other law-enforcement personnel against groups of protesters or demonstrators.

The Violence of Whites Against Blacks

Lynching mob "justice" is a thing of the past. But other forms of extreme aggression of whites against blacks remain. However, while the overall rate of violence by whites against blacks has steadily declined since the end of World War II, it still occurs regularly in all parts of the country. For example:

On January 8, 1967, in the small town of Brazelton, Georgia, 2 black men were refused service at a white-owned restaurant. Enraged that the blacks would even dare to test the Public Accommodations Section of the civil rights law, 25 white men rushed at them as they left the restaurant and beat them badly.

On May 30, 1967, a crowd of 100 white youths attacked a smaller group of blacks in a wooded section of a Chicago park, throwing rocks and bottles and seriously injuring twelve of them.

On July 2, 1967, at an integrated dance in Salt Lake City, white males became disturbed over the sight of African exchange students dancing with white Peace Corps workers. Some 100 white boys "ganged up on" the African students and beat them mercilessly.

The Violence of Blacks Against Whites

During the 1960s, the most frequently reported form of collective violence was that of blacks against whites. The President's

Commission on Civil Disorders examined some 160 incidents of black rioting in 1967, classifying 5 percent as "major," 20 percent as "serious," and 75 percent as "minor." In 1968, the number of incidents rose sharply, most incidents (125) occurring during the two weeks following the death of Martin Luther King, Jr.

Although the rate of violence by blacks against whites seems to be climbing out of proportion to the rate of white violence against blacks, there is a major difference between the two: white violence is directed primarily against people. The white racist wants to maim, cripple, or kill the black man. By contrast, black violence against whites is almost always directed against objects, that is, symbols of the white power structure: white-owned property or white-operated businesses and shops.

THE VIOLENCE OF POLICE AGAINST DEMONSTRATORS

Violence of the local and state police, National Guard, and other law-enforcing agencies is always supposed to be to preserve order and to enforce the law. At the present time it has been directed mainly at black people, campus demonstrators, and youthful nonconformists such as hippies.

In June 1967, Boston police handled roughly a group of black women picketing a welfare office in the ghetto. Then, according to bystanders, suddenly and apparently without reason they clubbed black residents who had gathered in the street to help the women, beating even some of the ghetto leaders who were trying to break up the crowd.

In April, 1968, more than 1,000 New York City police entered the campus of Columbia University to remove student protestors who were occupying administration buildings. More than 130 persons were beaten and clubbed by the police—students, faculty, and newsmen alike.

The most famous case of all occurred in August 1968, outside the Democratic National Convention in Chicago. Literally millions of horrified television viewers watched police set upon hundreds of marching demonstrators and scores of newsmen and innocent bystanders.

The police are not unruly, disorganized mobs but are members of professional organizations. Yet their behavior, on these rare occasions, is not very different from that of spontaneous crowds of protesting students, black or white. Their behavior is still another example of collective violence by a group spurred on by fear and rage.

THE ORIGINS OF GROUP VIOLENCE

Collective violence is not as rational—and certainly not as well planned—as other forms of group aggression, such as a war or a Cosa Nostra killing; but it is also not haphazard or random. Collective violence is usually the final step in a long series of conflicts between two opposing groups.

The exact conditions which cause the final release of pent-up hate or fear or rage are not completely understood. But certain orderly patterns can be seen in every urban riot, in every clash between police and protestors or between students and school administration.

First, violence begins with a conflict over basic values. Though later there would be disagreement over the lottery procedure, early debate over the military draft was inspired basically by the conflict between democratic theory and reality.

The next step is the development of a set of hostile beliefs rooted in the conflict of values. For example, blacks generally feel the white "Establishment" is "out to get them." In the particular case of the draft, many blacks believe the laws are specifically written to protect young whites and kill off young blacks.

The third condition leading to an outburst of violence is a breakdown in communication between the two opposing groups. The hostile beliefs then become magnified and exaggerated because neither side in the conflict really knows much about the other. For example, until protesting students seized a building at Harvard, many faculty members had no idea how bitter and resentful students were toward university policies. When the trouble is between blacks and whites, the amount of misunderstanding and misinformation keeping them apart is even more excessive. It was brought to light, for example, that in the ghettos of Chicago many black children believe that black people make up 80 or 90 percent of the city's population.

The fourth step is a breakdown of social control. Faced with impending violence, community leaders or law-enforcement agencies do either too much or too little. Police may "over-react" repressively and cruelly as they did in Chicago, or they may do nothing at all.

Finally, a riot or any other kind of group violence needs a *triggering* event. Usually such an event or incident involves (1) an actual insult or injury to a group or one of its members, (2) a threat to the social status of the group, and/or (3) a severe frustration of the group's striving for higher status.*

Actually, the trigger may be a minor incident. The routine arrest of a black man for drunken driving apparently touched off the destructive Watts riot in 1965. And a hundred different riots might have a hundred different triggers. Therefore, the real cause of collective violence may be found in the deeper and more serious basic conflicts between values. These are the conflicts which strain social relations to the breaking point.

CONTRADICTIONS IN AMERICAN DEMOCRACY

Perhaps at the heart of most, if not all the social strain in American life is the conflict between democratic ideals and authoritarian practices. Despite the claims to be a democratic society, fair and equal to all, many individuals and groups are actually shut out from the democratic process. On the surface, the American system is supposed to be equalitarian, but in reality it is often the very opposite, that is, authoritarian. The American Revolution was a rejection of European aristocratic values which supposedly were wholly replaced by the theory that "all men are created free and equal."

But even the drafters of the Constitution saw this new nation as a kind of *limited democracy*. Despite claims to equality for all, the Founding Fathers specified that a citizen needed special qualifications to vote and to have a share in the power of the government. He had to be:

1. WHITE, *which meant that all reds, yellows, browns, and blacks were excluded;*

2. ANGLO-SAXON, *or of some related Northern European*

* See "The Where and When of Race Riots" in *Racial and Ethnic Relations* in this *Readings in Sociology* Series.

stock, *which meant that all Mediterraneans, Orientals, and Eastern Europeans were excluded;*

3. PROTESTANT, *which meant that all Catholics, Jews, Moslems, and others were excluded;*

4. MIDDLE CLASS *or higher, which meant that all poor people, working people, or those who did not own property were excluded;*

5. ADULT, *which meant that all young people were excluded;*

6. *And, finally,* MALE, *which meant that all women were excluded.*

The cycle of riots and violence in American life is really a history of attempts by these various excluded groups to break down the barriers carried over from England in colonial days and to replace them wholly by the democratic principles stated at the time of the Revolution.

RECONSTRUCTIVISTS AND NATIVISTS

In the broadest terms, those people who try to break down the barriers might be called *Reconstructivists* and those who try to keep the barriers up might be called *Nativists.*

Obviously, the Reconstructivists want to *reconstruct* American democracy to include themselves. Moreover, the Reconstructivists, be they Irish, Jews, blacks, or youths, also want to bring elements of their own culture—art, music, food, and dress—into American life as well. (Today's Reconstructivists make more of this last point than did the Reconstructivists of the last century.)

The Nativists, on the other hand, want to keep these intruders from joining the elite circle of democracy. They also want to preserve the "American way of life," that is, their conception of democracy's "pure, *native* form" as it existed at the time of the Revolution.

The Nativists see the new cultural contributions of the Reconstructivists as corrupting rather than enriching this old way of life. To them any vision of their country that does not fit that special image must be "un-American."

When hard-core Nativist and militant Reconstructivist meet, violence is very likely to result, as it has in the border areas between white and black neighborhoods, on the steps of college buildings, or in the streets of Chicago. However, the manner in which the two groups use violence is quite different.

The Objects of Violence

When Reconstructivist protesters break into violence, their attacks are usually directed against impersonal targets, such as machinery, buildings, or business establishments. Reconstructivists obstruct. They burn. They attack and destroy property. They invade the seats of power and they occupy territory. But the violence is all designed to disrupt established order, not to injure or kill human beings.

By contrast, Nativist violence usually is directed at people. Nativists, of course, draw their recruits from the social groups most threatened by Reconstructivist "upstarts." And the Nativists fear the rebels will destroy all that is sacred. Thus when Nativists resort to violence, it is directed at the demonstrators and is very likely to be sadistic, cruel, and excessive. The Nativists seek to intimidate, to scare, and to drive off the opposition leaders. For many Nativists, the best way to destroy the Reconstructivist movement is to kill certain individuals (Martin Luther King was one) and to injure so many others that the leaders will be discouraged and their followers will be too frightened to take further action.

Obviously, the current clashes between whites and blacks and the protests of youths of all colors can be described as struggles between Nativists and Reconstructivists. But what about police violence? Where does their behavior fit into this struggle?

The police are generally on the side of the Nativists for two reasons. First, they are sworn to uphold the law and order of the "Establishment" which the Reconstructivists are determined to change.

Second, and more important, the police are usually recruited from former Reconstructivist groups who have just recently knocked down the barriers of exclusion themselves. One of the strangest results of the American social struggle is the almost immediate conversion of the winners. In other words, the Reconstructivists of one season become the Nativists of the next. The reasons for this conversion are not clear, but the Irish and Italians who struggled so hard to be accepted in the social system are now among the groups most strongly resisting the entry of new people.* The working class, which had a long, bloody fight before it won the right to strike (the term "strike" is violent in its very name), is now complaining loudest about law and order, permissive youth, and the threat of black power. In fact, George Wallace, an unsuccessful presidential candidate in 1968 who embodied the Nativist tradition, drew much of his support from union members.

One may imagine, then, how the Irish, Italian, or Polish policeman of a working-class background must feel when he meets a black-skinned activist or a long-haired student militant wearing beads. In the eyes of the police this new breed of Reconstructivist is the embodiment of everything that is alien, evil, destructive, and un-American—almost nonhuman. So, ruling the Reconstructivists out of the human race, they seem to the Nativists as "animals," deserving of attack.

Despite the desperate measures of the Nativists, the Reconstructivists eventually win the battles. Throughout the history of the American people the barriers set up by the elite against most groups have collapsed. Each excluded group has its time of ripeness. For the Irish, the time was the 1850s. The time for labor was in the 1890s. Now, perhaps, the time for youth and blacks has come. However, the barriers fall at different speeds in different groups. And occasionally the barriers fall without any violence at all.

Women broke down some of the barriers keeping them from full rights as workers and citizens without resorting to violence—at least in the United States. (In England, women of the aristocracy in 1911 paraded, provoked the police, and rioted.) In 1800, a woman had no right to vote, to own property, to hold office, or to conduct a lawsuit. She was a nonperson. By 1920, through patience and perseverance, American women had won the right to vote and the road to full equality was ahead. Of course, women are still not on a completely equal footing with men. Even yet, some do not receive equal pay for equal work—equal,

* See "Irish and Yankees in a Factory" in *Racial and Ethnic Relations* in this *Readings in Sociology* Series.

that is, with men—and so the process of knocking down the barriers can be a long and tedious affair.

A CHANGE AND A CHANCE FOR THE FUTURE

The most recent cycle of violence may have already reached its peak. At least, the large, undirected, irrational explosions of the mid- and late-1960s seem to be over. The disturbances on college campuses and in the cities, when life and property were destroyed for no apparent purpose, now seem to be replaced by protests directed at more specific targets.

For example, during the early months of 1969, ghetto mothers in Boston stormed the state welfare agencies and disrupted department store credit offices in a specific protest over welfare aid. At Harvard, Columbia, Cornell, and other universities, the student disturbances seemed directed at real, tangible issues, ranging from Reserve Officers Training Corps on campus to the involvement of black students in the selection of courses.

Violence will probably persist as long as the Reconstructivist-Nativist struggle to reshape the democratic system persists. However, violence may grow less and eventually come to an end if Americans honestly face the need to re-evaluate their own self-image.

We insist we will not tolerate violence and reject it as a method of settling public questions; yet we continue to tolerate it. We describe our society as democratic though some groups are denied a full share of economic and political life on grounds of race, some on grounds of sex, some on grounds of ethnic origin (national background), and some on grounds of religion. Such systematic exclusion is an invitation to Nativists and Reconstructivists to "fight it out"—yet we continue to deny the facts.

The first step, therefore, to bring violence to an end is to recognize this real shortcoming in American society. Then, after admitting that power is not equally shared by all, the next step is to develop means for sharing power with those who are still excluded.

Life on Skid Row*

What prompts a person to become an inhabitant of Skid Row? Is it choice? Circumstances? Or is he just "no good"?

How would you describe a Skid Rower? What does alcohol, violence, and crime have to do with his life?

What is life like on Skid Row, and how do the people spend their time? Is there any sort of social structure or community?

After a man becomes a member of Skid Row, how does he view the part of society from which he came? Does he wish to return to it? What are the obstacles preventing his return?

One of the lumbering jobs I had was working on skid road. . . . Logs were split to make skids, and the fallen timbers were fastened to them by chains and then slid down the hill into the river. 'I had a tallow pot and a brush. My job was to grease the skids from the tallow pot. . . . When those of us who worked the north woods found ourselves in a place where the skids were greased . . . we began to talk about the "skid road." Of course, now it is called skid row.

—Chester E. Brown
Lumberjack

Almost every major American city has its Skid Row, a drab, dirty neighborhood of flop houses, cheap restaurants, saloons, secondhand clothing stores, pawnshops, and missions that cater to the down-and-outer, the bum, the drifter, and the alcoholic.

Skid Row has been a part of American urban life since the end of the Civil War when discharged veterans, refugees, immigrants, and other homeless people first began congregating in

* Adapted from "The Road to Skid Row" by Samuel E. Wallace, *Social Problems*, Vol. 16, No. 1 (Summer 1968), pp. 92–105; and from "The Bottle Gang" by Earl Rubington, *Quarterly Journal of Studies on Alcohol*, Vol. 29, No. 4 (December 1968), pp. 943–955. Reprinted by permission.

the dingy corners of our cities. In some towns, the neighborhood may have a picturesque or descriptive name—the Bowery, Lower Town, the Square, Madison Street, the Mission District, Beer Gulch—but they are all Skid Rows.

And Skid Row has one meaning to the outside, or "straight," world. For more than a century, Skid Row has meant the end of the line—the final fall for society's dropouts, the last retreat of the down-and-outer, the street of no return.

For most Americans there is no place lower than Skid Row —and no one lower than a Skid Row bum. Skid Rowers are considered the scum of the earth, society's outcasts—drunkards and derelicts, lawbreakers and losers.

Recent sociological research, however, pokes some holes in the popular image of the typical Bowery Bum. For example, not all Skid Rowers are alcoholics—only a third, and perhaps as few as a tenth, of Skid Rowers are true alcoholics.

Skid Rowers are not particularly lawless men either. In fact, a Skid Rower is a most peaceful and passive type who only wants to be left alone. His bouts with drinking and his chronic vagrancy, however, give him a record of repeated arrests.

And most Skid Rowers are not mental defectives. They obviously have deep emotional problems, but so do many people who have never seen Skid Row.

Most important, perhaps, Skid Row actually is not the "end of the line" in the worst sense. For the homeless and the rootless, Skid Row is a place they can at least call their own. Skid Row is a very special kind of community with its own standards and status system and its own recognizable culture.

In other words, the Skid Rower may be an outcast from American society, but he is also a full-fledged member of his own "outcast community." Some men simply stumble into this community by chance, but others actually seek it out. No matter how they arrive, all eventually find that Skid Row is a way of life.

THE ROAD TO SKID ROW

Skid Row is generally so repulsive and contrary to all normal standards of living that people do not just decide to join in the way they make other decisions, such as to sign up at the YMCA or to buy a house in a suburban development. Becoming a member of Skid Row usually occurs slowly and unconsciously in a series of distinguishable steps. These steps are described by Professor Samuel E. Wallace of Brandeis University. He knows well the Skid Rows of New York, Minneapolis, and San Francisco and stayed in one of them for nine months. His data come from his observations and from interviews with some 300 of the derelicts whom he met on Skid Row.

The first step for a potential Skid Rower is *dislocation*, the breaking of ties with his home and family and any stable manner of living.

Years ago, vast numbers of men, women, and children became separated from their homes and families simply because of their work. Many trades and crafts required young apprentices to travel for several years as "journeymen" learning their basic skills. Also, soldiers were often discharged many miles from their homes. Seamen went on voyages that lasted several years. Entertainers traveled the vaudeville circuit and toured the "tank towns" with road companies. And thousands of unskilled and semiskilled laborers drifted through the expanding West, laying rail and telegraph lines, building dams and river levees, cutting lumber, and harvesting seasonal crops. Some of these drifters eventually returned home, but many others settled in the homes they knew on the road—the "hobo jungles," the flop houses of the big cities where a man could rent a bed for a few cents a night.

Today, improved opportunities for employment have reduced the number of roving workers to a handful of specially skilled construction workers. Such a worker was Johnny Ring, once a skilled "high steel" worker who worked at steel construction at dizzy heights above the ground. At 54, Johnny was a heavy drinker, unmarried, unemployed, uneducated, and headed straight for Skid Row.

Moreover, Skid Row, before any national welfare programs existed, provided the only place to which the destitute, the aged, the diseased, and displaced could turn for shelter, a bed, and food. During the Great Depression of the 1930s, for example, many cities actually built their poorhouses, shelters, and relief stations in the Skid Row sections. This confined the poverty-stricken to these areas. It must be admitted that the city governments would have been violently opposed if they had tried to put the shelters and poorhouses anywhere else.

Today, federal and state welfare programs provide some relief for the old and poor without making them leave their old homes. However, for some men, such as James Connell, Skid Row is still the only place left. Connell, 67, was a city clerk for forty years. He and his wife hoped to move to the country after his retirement. Her long illness wiped out Connell's modest savings. Widowed and with only his tiny pension and Social Security, he could no longer afford his old apartment in a good neighborhood.

Unlike Ring and Connell, who are cut off from old ties by circumstances, is another type, the middle-class alcoholic who may deliberately cut himself off. George Banning, 43, a well-to-do accountant had a drinking problem. To conceal his drinking from family, friends, and employer, he sought out bars in the Skid Row section where he was unknown and where drunkenness was taken for granted.

The next step on the road to Skid Row for Ring, Connell, Banning, and others is *exposure* to the way of life. Actually *exposure* and *dislocation* occur almost simultaneously. Johnny Ring came into direct contact with many Skid Rows as he traveled across the country. It was here that he stayed between jobs and here that he often found his next assignment. Always a shy man, anyway, Johnny found himself cut off from the world outside of his construction camp or the Skid Rows. He forgot the patterns of life outside and grew painfully shy and awkward in the presence of women. Finally, his wanderings and his bachelorhood set him apart from a society that is centered on family. By the time he reached middle age, he knew only the Skid Row way of life.

Reliefer James Connell fell into a similar trap. Forced by lack of money to move into a cheap Skid Row rooming house, he was embarrassed by his new surroundings. The middle-class behavior which came naturally to him was not acceptable in this new neighborhood and to survive in peace and avoid ridicule he began to behave like his neighbors.

George Banning, too, as he frequented Skid Row bars more and more often, became more and more at ease with the people around him.

The next step for the Skid Row newcomer is *regular partici-pation*. Of course, many of them have shared the life of Skid Row already. Before, however, Johnny Ring, James Connell, and George Banning always held out hope that they would someday leave the neighborhood: Skid Row was just a temporary stop-over. Each could always produce "credentials" to prove that he was really "a skilled high-steel worker," or "a retired clerk down on his luck," or a "respected businessman fighting off a minor drinking problem."

As time passes, and Johnny, James, and George remain on Skid Row, only their fellow Skid Rowers believe their so-called "credentials." No one else helps them keep up the illusion. For to the outside world, all men living on Skid Row—including Johnny, James, and George—are "bums."

Every day, outsiders tell the Skid Rower he is no good, a failure, a misfit, a derelict. Finally, this pressure becomes too much to bear. The Skid Row newcomer starts to avoid contacts with the old world he once knew. He withdraws more and more into his new neighborhood. Indeed, he may turn the tables on his critics and begin calling outsiders foolish and ignorant. He may even glorify the Skid Row way of life to justify his own existence.

The final step, then, is full *integration* into Skid Row. The newcomer masters the special slang. He replaces family, friends, and neighbors entirely with Skid Row acquaintances. Johnny Ring stops working and wandering and settles down to a round of "panhandling" (begging) and drinking. James Connell for-gets his embarrassment over standing in line for relief checks and eats all his meals in cheap restaurants rather than going down-town. George Banning's visits to the Skid Row bars grow longer and longer until one day he simply fails to sober up and go home.

From the point of view of outsiders, Johnny, James, and George have become completely "desocialized." But, from the point of view of their fellow Skid Rowers, they have finally be-come members of the community, insiders who belong.

Once accepted on Skid Row, these newcomers will occupy a status in the community recognized only by Skid Rowers. Very simply, the Skid Row hierarchy is the complete opposite of that in the outside world: the lower you are in the eyes of the public, the higher you are in the Skid Row community! Making progress on Skid Row's social ladder means working your way down—getting farther and farther away from the outsiders' idea of conformity and propriety.

SKID ROW STATUS

Johnny Ring ranks at the top of the Skid Row social scale because he became a drunk!

But to be a drunk on Skid Row does not mean to be an alcoholic. True alcoholics usually drink alone and with no other thought than to become intoxicated as soon as possible. The alcoholic does not need other people—only his bottle.

Not so the Skid Row "drunk." Heavy drinking on Skid Row is a group activity. The typical "drunk" is a member of a "bottle gang," which decides on the time, place, and amount of drinking, and indeed even on the behavior of the drinkers.

Professor Earl Rubington, then a sociologist at Rutgers, University's Center of Alcohol Studies, described the bottle gang in detail. He studied it by the method which sociologists call "participant observation." As a participant observer, Professor Rubington mingled freely with the men at a rehabilitation center for alcoholics. He went there day after day for months, familiarizing himself with the men, their attitudes, and their ways. For their part, the men whom he observed understood he was a sympathetic student of their problems and gave him their confidence. From what he saw and heard, the sociologist arrived at the following description of the bottle gang:

On a typical day, Johnny Ring might go to the park or some other central point where the drinkers gather and join his fellow drunkards in a set ritual of drinking that is governed by strict rules of etiquette. Each move is set by convention and one move follows another in a set order.

1. *The salutation.* Potential bottle-gang members meet and greet each other. They sit on a bench, pass the time of day, and share information about old buddies. Here the rules are simple: never snub a drinking man and treat everyone as an equal.

2. *Negotiation.* Each man knows the others are, as they put it, "on the prowl" in search of a drink. Someone, perhaps Johnny,

starts the negotiations by saying he has a certain amount of money to contribute toward the price of a bottle. ("I have eighteen cents. How much are you holding?") If they have too little money for a bottle, the leader may invite other members in or panhandle for a bit. The rules are clear: buy or work your way into the gang—"don't chisel in."

3. *Procurement.* When the little group has enough cash ("made the price" or "scored"), the leader chooses one man "to make the run" and buy the bottle. The runner usually is the least shabbily dressed, the most sober, and the most dependable, that is, he can be trusted to return. The rest of the gang sits quietly and waits patiently, for that, too, is part of the ritual.

4. *Consumption.* The runner returns with the bottle—usually cheap muscatel wine—in a brown paper bag hidden under his coat. He gives it to the leader. The leader quickly looks about for the police, then breaks the seal, takes two short drinks, and passes it back to the runner who gets the next "swig." The bottle, still in its paper bag, then goes around the circle. The last man gives it back to the leader. Drinking is controlled by the most serious rules: let the leader split the seal and take the first drinks; wait your turn and then match his drinks; take two and pass the bottle; do not let the world see you drinking.

5. *Affirmation* (or socializing). After the first round, the men usually sit back and relax, light up cigarettes and chat. The leader sets the tone and topics of conversation. There is little talk of personal problems and much of the troubles of others. Everyone speaks disapprovingly of outsiders and of "drunks" who have broken bottle-gang rules, for example, men who have run off with the bottle, or who drank more than their share, or caused the gang to be arrested by his loud behavior. Each man affirms that this is a "good gang of guys."

6. *Dispersal.* The leader decides when the last round of the bottle takes place. Again, it travels the circle, with each man taking two drinks. When the bottle is empty, the gang is ready to disperse. The man holding the bottle last, disposes of it—still in its brown bag—in a trash barrel or under a bench. Of course, any member could start a new cycle of bottle-buying and drinking, or the group could simply disband. Getting rid of the bottle not only removes the evidence and reduces the risk of arrest; it

also signifies that the gang may break up now. All rights and duties of the gang are now officially ended. The men are, for the time being, free of each other's company.

The bottle-gang perhaps is the most important type of group on Skid Row. Most heavy drinkers take part in its ritual. It is unlikely, however, that true alcoholics such as George Banning could go through such an elaborate performance just to get a drink. George would share neither drinks nor funds. He indulges in solitary drinking bouts. And, strangely enough, he and the other true alcoholics keep some of the outside world's attitudes toward the Skid Row drunkard. Perhaps because of his relatively higher status in pre-Skid Row days, he does not like to think of himself as a common "drunk."

However, in the public's eyes—and on police blotters—there is little distinction between drunkard and alcoholic. Both are arrested and jailed together, both spend long hours in bars, both panhandle, and both seem to sacrifice everything for the sake of a drink. But on Skid Row there is a difference between the two. The "drunk" is part of the group. The alcoholic, still retaining a bit of the outside world's aloofness, is slightly lower in status.

Another step down the status scale is the "hobo." Once, particularly at the turn of the century, hobos made up the largest proportion of Skid Row, which often was called "Hobohemia." Fine distinctions were made between the hobos (who worked and wandered), the tramps (who dreamed and wandered), and the bums (who drank and wandered). True hobos would be insulted if called tramps or bums.

Hobos had their own songs, traditions, tales, and even organizations such as the "Hobo College" and the IWW (International Workers of the World), the famous laborers' union, better known as the "Wobblies."

Today, the true hobos—migrant workers—have generally disappeared and the term is applied to anyone who wanders continuously through Skid Rows because of his work, wanderlust, or fear of the law. Johnny Ring was a typical hobo for many years before he worked his way up (or down) the social ladder by becoming a bottle-gang drunk.

"Beggars" occupy the fourth status level—although not all beggars live on Skid Row. The beggar's success depends on his talents as an actor, psychologist, and diplomat, and his trade should not be confused with simple panhandling. In Skid Row terms, panhandling takes places between equals, and the bottle-gang drinker who gets money from fellow drunks looks down on the beggar who grovels before outsiders. Even among beggars there is a subsystem of status which ranges from the man who begs money on the street down to the "scavenger" who paws through garbage pails and trash bins.

Just below the beggars comes the "tour director," who is a master "con artist" specializing in "putting on the tourists."

The tour directors usually are the wanderers, the dreamers, and the disenchanted among those who have landed on Skid Row. Somehow, they have taken over responsibility for entertaining all visitors. Smart enough to know what their listeners want to hear, they spin tragic personal life histories which they know will earn them a drink. It is probably the tour directors who have conned journalists and authors into believing many of the legends about Skid Row—for example, the myth that Skid Row is populated by alcoholic brain surgeons, defrocked priests, dope-crazed artists, and embezzling bank presidents is mainly the creation of imaginative tour directors.

The final and lowest status groups on Skid Row are the "mission stiffs" and the "reliefers," such as James Connell. The first group depends on religious missions and the second group on public welfare agencies for their support. The high-status drinker who has no contact with the outside world except through a jail looks down on these men and women. They are considered to be in sympathy with the values of the outside world, not with Skid Row's values. Moreover, many reliefers—James Connell is one—merely use the cheap facilities of Skid Row without participating in such institutions as the bottle-gang.

Obviously, acceptance on Skid Row, as in other communities, depends greatly on one's loyalty and association with fellow members. The loyalty of the "drunk" is unquestioned because of his conformity to the bottle-gang rules. The alcoholic ranks high in status because of his prodigious drinking but is less respected because of his superior background and closer contacts in the outside world (he is more likely than the other Skid Row men to have been married and had children) plus his refusal to join in group drinking. The hobo who works damages his status because he keeps in contact with employers on the outside and because he does not maintain permanent residence on Skid Row.

The beggar, too, must approach outsiders and often bow to their demands. Thus, he "degrades" the Skid Row way of life. Similarly, the tour director actually talks to outsiders and may betray Skid Row standards by attracting public attention to other members. Finally, the mission stiffs and reliefers are disloyal because they actively support agencies and organizations which threaten the safety of Skid Row life.

These are the standards by which Skid Rowers judge each other. They are standards unknown—and unbelievable—to most middle-class Americans. Yet, those who have status on Skid Row cherish and protect them.

Of course, the particular status hierarchy of the Bowery or Madison Street or any Skid Row may change from day to day. Arrests, deaths, intrusions by outsiders, and the seasonal or even weekly and daily movements of the inhabitants constantly upset the delicate balance of this local society. Nevertheless, Skid Row life in the United States is just as real today as it was in the 1870s.

THE FUTURE OF SKID ROW

But time seems to be running out for Skid Row society. Progress and urban renewal apparently have doomed this strange community to extinction.

The changing economics of American life has contributed to the decline of Skid Row populations. The old lumbering, construction, and farm work camps from which potential Skid Rowers were recruited have generally disappeared. Farming and lumbering, now largely mechanized, are no longer great employers of men. New welfare policies provide relief without putting people into Skid Row shelters or poorhouses. Full employment and better job opportunities provide steady jobs for all but the most seriously ill or unfit.

During the Depression, a national census of homeless men and women totaled more than one million. Today, that total has dropped to less than 100,000, with most of them over 50 years old. According to a survey made by Columbia University's Bureau of Applied Social Research along New York City's Bowery, the annual head counts of flop houses and rescue missions show a steady decline of about 5 percent per year. Between 1949 and 1967, the Bowery population fell from 13,675 to 4,580. By 1975, social workers expect the number to drop below 2,500.

After a long, rich history in which literally millions of persons have come and gone, Skid Row at last appears ready to fade from the American scene.

Drugs and Drug Users*

Does drug use by itself cause human beings to engage in crime or violence?

What are differences between individuals who use illicit drugs and engage in crime and those who use the same drugs but who do not commit crimes?

Are there differences in the risks of crime depending upon the type of drug which has been used?

How do the effects of an approved drug such as alcohol differ from the effects of disapproved (illicit) drugs?

In the first ten weeks of 1970, 51 teen-agers, an average of five a week, died of heroin in New York City. One of them was ten years old. In 1969, when 224 New York teen-agers died as a result of drug-taking, the average was four a week. It is probably true already that one teen-ager dies of drugs every day in New York. Other big cities may not equal New York's record—yet—but week by week drug use is growing more common and more dangerous.

In 1965, Dr. Timothy Leary, a psychologist-prophet, was reported in the newspapers to be urging his audiences to "turn on, tune off, and drop out." His words have since become as familiar to most Americans as Horace Greeley's one-time admonition, "Go West, young man." Like Greeley, Dr. Leary was something of a pioneer, though the "trip" he advertised had little in common with either the pace or purpose of 19th-century travel.

What Leary offered instead was a journey into the interior of the mind—to be made, conveniently enough, without benefit of maps, movement, or money. It was, as he described it, a magical

* Adapted from "Drugs, Behavior, and Crime" by Richard H. Blum, *Annals of the American Academy of Political and Social Science*, Vol. 374 (November 1967), pp. 135–146. Reprinted by permission.

mystery tour. Leary was, of course, promoting LSD, a powerful hallucinogenic drug (one which brings on hallucinations) that alters perception and expands consciousness.

Whether Dr. Leary contributed in any real way to the unprecedented rise in drug usage in the United States during the 1960s or whether he should be considered a symptom rather than a cause is an urgent but unanswered question.

There is certainly nothing new about taking drugs which affect the senses and the mind, changing, for example, the sensations of sight and of sound and the sense of time and space.

The Chinese have used opium for thousands of years to achieve relaxation, forgetfulness, or a sense of well-being. From China, opium spread to Europe, brought by the early traders. About 150 years ago, opium became a fad among a small group of English writers and painters and one of them, Thomas De-Quincey, wrote *The Confessions of an English Opium Eater*, a book which became famous. The Mexicans were taking peyote before Europeans first landed in the New World. Other peoples have used drugs in religious ceremonies, as the drug hashish is used today in India. If the hippies in American cities experiment with marijuana, LSD, "speed," "pep pills," and other drugs, they are copying behavior that is virtually world-wide and known for thousands of years. They are not doing anything new.

What is new today is that drug-taking is greatly on the increase and that it is spreading among classes of people who did not use drugs before and are, on the whole, much younger than the drug users of the generations before them. In the decade of the 1960s, drug-taking changed from a purely underground activity to a pastime shared by young people and the middle class. It has become an important element in the "youth culture." °

There are, of course, many people who take drugs prescribed for them by doctors. Such lawful use does not concern us here; we are interested in self-prescribed illicit use. Estimates of the number who have taken drugs, on their own, at one time or another, range from a conservative 5 million to highs of 12 million or even 20 million Americans. At least two hundred thousand of these users are considered heavily dependent. If alcoholics are

° See "Middle-Class Delinquency" in this book.

included the number rises to nearly 7 million. Not only are more and more people taking drugs; more and more people are talking about them, preaching about them, writing about them, and sometimes even singing about them.

As a behavioral scientist with a special interest in the fields of mental health, drugs, and crime, Richard H. Blum, of Stanford University's Institute for the Study of Human Problems, tackles this whole issue squarely. He has drawn upon his familiarity with drugs and their users gained in years of professional concern with the subject and in service as a consultant to the President's Committee on Law Enforcement and the Administration of Justice. This is what he reports is reliably known about drugs.

DRUGS AND BEHAVIOR

Heroin, morphine, barbiturates, amphetamines, LSD, marijuana, alcohol—all are powerful agents which can affect the mind, the mood, the biological cycles, the energy levels, and the interpersonal relations of those who use them. These agents are conventionally grouped into classes, as, for example, narcotics, sedatives, tranquilizers, stimulants, antidepressants, hallucinogens (which cause hallucinations), and intoxicants. The classifications are based on the most probable effects of the drugs.

But these labels are overlapping and inexact, at best. For example, alcohol, an intoxicant, can, in addition, be classified as a depressant, as a tranquilizer, or as a stimulant, depending on its effects on different individuals or its different effects at different stages of its consumption. It is also capable of producing hallucinations, as in delirium tremens. Likewise, marijuana is considered by some to be an intoxicant, by others, an hallucinogen, and at law, a narcotic—although medically the term "narcotic" properly refers only to drugs which are derived from opium. Again, heroin, a narcotic, and LSD, an hallucinogen, may also be called euphoriants (substances producing a sense of happiness or well-being), even though many people are made ill or are confused and upset by them.

Drug-influenced behavior is actually far from predictable. It can only be thought of in terms of probabilities. Among the many factors determining the nature of drug-induced behavior are: the amount of dosage taken, how the drug is administered, how often it is taken, the bodily state of the person using it, and the presence (or absence) in his body of chemical substances which might counteract or enhance the drug's effects. Other factors which influence a drug-taker's conduct are his personality, his expectations and emotions, and the environment in which he takes the drug. For instance, a suggestible person who is given a neutral substance which he mistakenly believes to be a powerful drug may actually react quite dramatically: he may break out in a rash, or vomit, or his blood pressure may soar. Or he may feel pain or disability less keenly than at other times. And, similarly, someone who has had the real thing may "feel" what he thinks he is supposed to feel.

If the use of the drug is institutionalized in a formal way, as in religious rituals or festivals, an individual's reactions will probably be more formal, or patterned. But if it is used in an informal setting, such as at a party or casual gathering where there are fewer restraining conventions and rituals, individual behavior will vary more. In other words, both the setting of use and the intentions of the user influence an individual's reactions to a drug. Furthermore, the same drug may be used by different people in an attempt to produce quite different effects.

WHY DO PEOPLE USE DRUGS?

There are possibly as many answers to this question as there are individual users. Generally it is for one or more of the following reasons: for "kicks"; from curiosity; because others in the crowd are doing so; to help get over shyness or to break down social barriers; to explore or gain insight into oneself; to heighten a religious experience; to prove one's manhood; to defy authority; to lighten physical or mental pain; or to compensate for personal failure or frustration.* But the reasons a person may have for taking a drug for the first time are often quite different from the reasons he has for continuing its use, and, further, the reasons for

---

* See "The Slum: Opportunities for Crime and Delinquency" in this book; also "Cats, Kicks, and Color" in *Cities and City Life* in this *Readings in Sociology* Series.

continuing use may be different from the reasons either for stopping, or being unable to stop.

For example, a 16-year-old Puerto Rican boy from Spanish Harlem may initially take heroin for this complex of reasons: (1) he has previously experimented illicitly with marijuana and so has become used to the idea; (2) heroin is readily available from pushers in the streets of the slums; (3) an older acquaintance persuades him to try the dangerous drug by appealing to his sense of "machismo" (manliness) and his unwillingness to appear "chicken"; and (4) he may already be accustomed to delinquency, so that it does not lie heavily on his conscience to go one step further.

But after continuing this "social" use, the boy may find that he feels better, not only because of the sense of well-being the heroin produces in him, but because the drug dispels his anxiety about the future and helps him to forget his present poverty and his unhappy family life. But at the same time that he is discovering his *psychological dependency* on the drug (that is, his persistent need or craving for it), he also finds that his system has become more tolerant of it. In other words, after repeated use, he finds that he has to keep taking more to obtain the original "happy" effects. Later, when he realizes that it is no longer possible to reach the happy state, no matter how much he takes, he may just continue the doses and get whatever comfort he can from them. Or he may try to blot out awareness altogether.

On the other hand, if he tries at this point to break the habit, the chances are that he will not be able to, that he has, in fact, become "hooked" (addicted). He will find that he is now *physically dependent*, as well as psychologically dependent on the drug. Habitual use has so altered his bodily state that whenever he has to go without the drug he suffers nausea or acute pain. Therefore, to escape the terrors of "withdrawal sickness," he will probably start in again on the drug, though this time his motive for using it will be simply to avoid the pain that the addiction to the drug has caused.

In contrast, consider how different the drug experience of a 20-year-old college student may be. In his dormitory or at some off-campus party he may be introduced almost by accident to "pot" (marijuana), LSD, or some other "mind-bending" drug popular with the psychedelic generation. Originally out of curiosity, mixed with some vague desire for strange or thrilling experience, he may later continue to use one or more of the drugs for another reason: because it quiets his worries over his studies, his career, or the draft, because it helps him relax from pressure, because it shows he is an accepted member in a world of his peers, or simply because he enjoys drug use.

After he graduates and takes a job in the "square" world, however, he may drop the practice altogether. He may switch from drugs to the more conventional alcohol for his "highs," in order to conform to the habits of an older generation and out of a growing fear of breaking the law. Or he may not turn to alcohol at all. In other words, this young man's use of drugs is a temporary habit that can be taken up or abandoned at convenience, with no question of addiction.

However, some other youth, because of his personal problems or maladjustment to life and his much greater psychological need of escape, may find it much more difficult (or may not even have the desire) to break the drug habit. Furthermore, he may be unlucky enough to have picked for his poison one of the narcotics or sedative-hypnotics which are definitely known to be habit-forming.

DAMAGE TO THE DRUG USER

Two basic assumptions underlie the laws against the drug traffic: (1) that drugs, when not prescribed by a doctor, are harmful to individual users; and (2) that persons taking drugs are led to act in ways that are harmful to others. Just how valid are these assumptions? Dr. Blum went into the evidence which backs up these assumptions. First of all, he asked, what are the dangers of various drugs to the individual? This is how he summarizes the available evidence.

1. Most users, whether one-time or periodic, of most mind-altering drugs do not appear to suffer damage to their health or in their personal adjustment. However, the likelihood of damage increases as larger amounts of the drugs are consumed over longer periods of time. There are some notable exceptions to this general rule: One-time overdoses of morphine, barbiturates, and

other mind-affecting substances can cause death. One-time users of LSD can suffer psychotic (mental) breakdowns. On the other hand, if occasional, or social, drinking is combined with proper nutrition and hygiene, the lifelong use of alcohol need not necessarily be dangerous.

2. Damaging physical or psychological effects vary depending on the condition of the person. His condition, in turn, is a product of his social and medical history. Statistically, the one group most likely to suffer the ill effects of heroin dependency (as well as alcoholism) are poor males who live in large cities. Other high-risk groups are those with a greater exposure to drugs and a greater opportunity to use them in informal settings. Examples are physicians and nurses, who have easy access to the opiates in their cabinets, and patients who have been prescribed very large quantities of barbiturates or tranquilizers by their doctors.

3. How much damage is done by using drugs also seems to depend on how the user has learned to use drugs. For example, just as young people who are taught the use of alcohol at home are less likely to become alcoholics than those who learn to drink with the street-corner gang, so patients who are "taught" the use of morphine in a hospital are less likely to grow dependent on the drug than slum adolescents who have been taught by older peers.

4. Damage is probably closely related to the reason for using the drug. For instance, persons indulging in self-medication to "escape," to solve problems, or to reduce anxiety seem to run greater risks than those individuals who use drugs to gain social sense, or to heighten religious rituals, or to treat a specific medical problem.

5. Mind-affecting drugs, without known exception, pose potential dangers. For example: about 1 out of every 14 to 20 (between 5 and 7 percent) alcohol users becomes an alcoholic (there are probably 6 million of them in the United States). Of LSD users, an estimated 3 percent become psychotic (beyond the period of the "trip" itself); still other LSD "trippers" injure themselves seriously during the period of hallucinations brought on by the drug. Whether LSD also has harmful long-term effects on the structure of genes is still completely unknown. We cannot say if the children of LSD users will be born defective until more

research is done. No one knows how many barbiturate users become disabled, but such drugs do create great physical dependence. There is increasing evidence that the chronic use of amphetamines ("speed") in large quantities for the purpose of getting "stoned" can bring on psychotic states. However, there is no sure evidence, at present, that marijuana taken in moderation causes ill effects.

As for heroin, nearly all who use it on a regular basis become addicted, and users are dying from it in increasingly larger numbers and at ever younger ages. In 1966 in New York, 33 teenagers died after taking heroin. In 1968, it was 72. And in June, July, and August alone in 1969, the number was 71. Of these, 60 percent were black and 30 percent were Puerto Rican. The New York City police report that 14-year-old addicts are "not uncommon." In New York City in January 1970, a 10-year-old boy was found dead after using heroin, and children as young as eight years of age have been discovered to be taking the drug.

Dr. Blum, in the same way, summarizes the facts already known to answer the second assumption: Do drugs actually "cause" crime or in any way lead users to commit violent or other antisocial acts? Certainly, many people trace the spiraling crime rates * in the country to the even faster spiraling drug usage rates. Governor Rockefeller, for one, has made public the estimate that perhaps half the reported crime in New York is the work of addicts. Dr. Blum, however, believes that positive evidence linking drug use to dangerous behavior is inadequate. The belief that drugs cause crime results from the lack of data on the drug-use habits of offenders and nonoffenders and from the failure to consider the total life-pattern of persons committing offenses and the role drugs play in their lives.

This is what Dr. Blum finds can be safely stated:

1. There is a strong link between the use of alcohol and the occurrence of automobile accidents. Alcoholics, in particular, account for a disproportionate share of auto accidents.

2. There is no evidence that the use of other drugs is strongly associated with accidents. However, driving skill can be reduced by depressant drugs and by marijuana.

* See "Crime Waves: The Record of 120 Years in Boston" in this book.

3. There is evidence that drugs are often an essential part of life among criminals. However, persons identified as "addicts" have usually already had records of delinquency *before* being arrested on narcotics charges. The evidence further suggests that adolescents who use unpredictable intoxicants, such as amphetamine-barbiturate mixes and the like, are often involved in other forms of delinquent behavior. Marijuana, on the other hand, is used both by slum adolescents with delinquent histories and by college students and successful professionals not otherwise connected with crime.

4. Whether heroin influences later criminality is not clear. Since, before the first heroin experience, the user is already likely to be a delinquent, associating with other delinquents, heroin cannot be assumed to "cause" his crime. However, the cost of maintaining this expensive habit may lead him to more and more stealing. "Hooked" customers in New York City often must pay $30 or more a day to feed the "monkey on their backs." But there is no evidence to show that heroin users steal more than their delinquent peers who do not use heroin. In fact, addicts in many cases do not have the ability to plan and execute very complicated crimes. However, addicts released after treatment who return to drug use *do* commit more crimes than released addicts who do not resume heroin use.

5. There is reason to believe that drugs, particularly alcohol, play a part in crimes of violence. But here again, those who commit such crimes while "under the influence" are likely to have had lifelong histories of unruly behavior, personal difficulties, impaired judgment, and delinquency. On rare occasions, psychotic reactions to amphetamines, hallucinogens, or marijuana may also produce violent behavior.

CONCLUSION

In view of what he has learned about drugs and those who take them, Dr. Blum feels that public concern which focuses on the dangers of drugs without also focusing on the drug-user himself is misdirected. It is, after all, a person who employs a drug, and a person who either harms himself or harms others as a result of drugs. Therefore, it is the person who must be studied and it is the reasons for and the consequences of his use of drugs that need to be established.

Statistically, the persons most likely to be harmed or to do harm to others because of drugs are those who already suffer a variety of other deprivations, miseries, and deficiencies—primarily big-city slum-dwelling males. Among them the minority groups are overrepresented, for they are often among the most disadvantaged. These groups are also overrepresented in crimes in the street. Thus, in Dr. Blum's opinion, it would be useful to consider such drug abuse as but one of many expressions of distress or disorder in the life of the user.

Knowing the statistical connection between drug abuse and crime, on the one hand, and inferior education and the environment of the typical urban ghetto, on the other, Dr. Blum recommends that, until these evils are abolished, we turn to a temporary solution. It is the continued control of the distribution of drugs, plus a more charitable, individually oriented administration of the current drug laws, and the treatment of drug-takers as sick people rather than as criminals. In many American cities alcoholics are now given medical and psychiatric help, instead of being thrown into jail and fined. The same attitude toward drug-takers might, as with alcoholics, prove a step toward their rehabilitation.

Suggested Reading

The most popular books on crime are detective stories. But in detective novels the story is the hunt for the doer of the deed, and as a rule the detective is the hero. Sherlock Holmes and James Bond and other famous heroes of the hunt are the "good" guys; the criminal is the "bad" guy. (Perhaps that is why detective stories are almost never about juvenile delinquency: we do not like to cast a young person in the role of the "bad" guy.)

But the sociologist is not interested in the chase to find the offender. He wants to find out why, while *most* people observe the law, there are always some who break it. Therefore, his interest is in the delinquent and the criminal *as persons,* and in crime itself as a normal (in the sense of being expected) aspect of social life, for in every human society there are individuals who break the law.

The reading list which follows is in two sections. The first section contains works which are written to interest and entertain the reader. They are often founded on an actual event, as, for example, Capote's *In Cold Blood.* This is the true story of the murder of a family of four, the discovery of the two murderers, and an account of their childhood and adult lives. It is a detective story which interests us because it is also a case history. From such a tale the reader can begin to understand how some men come to commit brutal crimes. But other books on the list are works of pure fiction. In them the author supplies by his imagination the circumstances and experiences which help to explain a criminal deed. That is what makes such works of fiction interesting even to a scientist.

In the second section are reports of scientific research undertaken by social scientists who specialize in the study of delinquency and crime. Like a novelist the sociologist may use imagination. He needs imagination in forming his hypotheses. But the sociologist's imagination is checked and disciplined by scientific method. As a result, he should end with statements with which another sociologist, in going over the same evidence, would agree.

A few articles, for example the study of murderers by Marvin E. Wolfgang, have no clear bearing on any particular selection. But they are included because they are interesting in themselves and may introduce fascinating side issues.

A. BIOGRAPHY, FICTION, AND JOURNALISTIC ACCOUNTS

Capote, Truman, *In Cold Blood*. New York: Random House, Inc., 1965. (Also a Signet paperback.)
The true story of two murderers of a family of four in 1959 in Kansas; their childhood and family life, aspirations, adolescence, and finally their trial and execution, five years after the crime. (6, 7)

Hellman, Lillian, *The Little Foxes*. New York: The Viking Press, Inc., 1968.
A play about the conspiracy of two avaricious brothers in the South to cheat their sister and her husband in a crooked business deal; and the sister's retaliation. (10)

Hughes, Helen MacGill, ed., *The Fantastic Lodge: The Autobiography of a Girl Drug Addict*. New York: Houghton Mifflin Company, 1961. (Also a Fawcett Premier paperback.)
The life story of a girl addicted at the age of 18 and dead by suicide at 23; how she got the habit, and what her life as an addict was like. (20)

Maas, Peter, *The Valachi Papers*. New York: Bantam Books, Inc. (paperback.)
The edited papers of a member of the Mafia who, in 1964, became an informer and revealed the structure of the Cosa Nostra. (16, 17)

Paton, Alan, *Too Late the Phalarope*. New York: Charles Scribner's Sons, 1953.
A young Afrikaner police officer, offending against South Africa's racial laws, ruins himself and his pious family. (10)

Reynolds, Frank, *Freewheelin' Frank: Secretary of the Angels*. New York: Grove Press, Inc., 1967.
The story of the Hell's Angels by a member of the gang. (6, 7)

Williamson, Henry, *Hustler!* New York: Doubleday and Company, Inc., 1965.
A personal account of a lower-class criminal in Chicago, with commentary by an anthropologist. (5, 6, 7)

B. RESEARCH STUDIES

Alexander, C. Norman, "Alcohol, Crime and Adolescent Rebellion," *Social Forces*, Vol. 46, No. 4 (June 1967), pp. 542–550.

A study of 1410 male high school seniors shows adolescent drinking is associated with lack of love between the boy and his father. (6, 15, 20)

Bauer, E. Jackson, "The Trend of Juvenile Offenders in the Netherlands and the United States," *Journal of Criminal Law, Criminology, and Police Science*, Vol. 55 (1964), pp. 359–369.

A study connecting rates of juvenile delinquency in Holland and in the United States with other social conditions. (14)

Bell, Daniel, "Crime as an American Way of Life," *Antioch Review*, Vol. 13 (Summer 1953), pp. 146–151.

Throughout American history, the foreign-born were powerless in politics and business, but some gained power in illegitimate enterprises (racketeering, etc.). In time each ethnic group gained access to legitimate ways to power and the later arrivals took their place in underworld activity, graft, and the rackets. (15, 16, 17)

Block, Herbert, "The Sociology of Gambling," *American Journal of Sociology*, Vol. 57, No. 3 (November 1951), pp. 215–221.

In societies where individuals gain their status in competition, and success largely depends upon money and possessions, the temptation is great to "take a chance." (7)

Caplan, Nathan S., and Paige, Jeffrey, "A Study of Ghetto Rioters," *Scientific American*, Vol. 219, No. 2 (August 1968), pp. 15–21.

A study of the Newark and Detroit riots shows it was *not* the poorest, nor the uneducated, nor the unemployed blacks who rioted. (18)

Chilton, Richard, and Spielberger, Adele, "Is Delinquency Increasing?" *Social Forces*, Vol. 49, No. 3 (March, 1971), pp. 487–493.

Analysis of Florida statistics reveals that much of the apparent increase in delinquency is accounted for by the increase of children of the ages when delinquency is most frequent. (4)

Clinard, Marshall B., "The Relationship of Urbanization and Urbanism to Criminal Behavior," in Burgess, Ernest W., and Bogue, Donald J., ed., *Contributions to Urban Sociology*. Chicago: University of Chicago Press, 1964, pp. 541–558.

Shows that in the United States and Sweden the great cities have the highest crime rates, then smaller cities, with farm and rural communities having the lowest rates; with theories to explain this. (15)

Cohen, Albert K., *Delinquent Boys: The Culture of the Gang*. New York: The Free Press, 1955.

The gang has a culture of its own, lives by it, and does not conform to the values of society. Within the culture the members carry on the legitimate search for a mode of life, but by unacceptable means. (5, 6, 7, 8)

Coles, Robert, *The Grass Pipe*. Boston: Little, Brown and Company, 1969.
Written for teen-agers to tell what marijuana is, why young people take it, and what makes them find it attractive. (20)

Conant, Ralph W., "Rioting, Insurrection and Civil Disobedience," *The American Scholar*, Vol. 37, No. 3 (Summer 1968), pp. 420–433.
A study of (1) precondition of rioting, (2) riot phases, and (3) social control of rioting; with discussion of conditions under which nonviolent and violent civil disobedience are tolerated. (18)

Cowie, John; Cowie, Valerie; and Slater, Eliot, *Delinquency in Girls*. New York: Humanities Press, Inc., 1968.
Delinquency in girls in England since 1950; differences in delinquent behavior of boys and girls; poverty and deprivation in the lives of girl and boy delinquents. (4, 5, 6, 7)

Cressey, Donald R., and Volkman, Rita, "Differential Association and the Rehabilitation of Drug Addicts," *American Journal of Sociology*, Vol. 69, No. 2 (September 1963), pp. 129–142.
A description of a rehabilitation center for addicts, built according to sociological concepts of the addicts' social world. (20)

Davis, Fred, "Focus on the Flower Children: Why All of Us May be Hippies Some Day," *Trans-action*, Vol. 5, No. 2 (December, 1967), pp. 10–18.
Interpretation of hippie values and hippie solutions to problems of marriage and family, consumption, poverty, passive spectator sports, etc., as advance solutions to problems which society must face. (9)

Feagin, Joe R., and Sheatsly, Paul B., "Ghetto Resident Appraisals of a Riot," *Public Opinion Quarterly*, XXXII, No. 3 (Fall, 1968), pp. 352–362.
Report of an inquiry among 200 blacks after a riot in Harlem, New York, into their reasons for being on the scene. (18)

Flacks, Richard, "Young Intelligentsia in Revolt," *Trans-action*, Vol. 7, No. 8 (June, 1970), pp. 47–55.
Analysis of trends among middle-class youth which converged just when the population of young people was at its greatest, with the effect of turning a small, alienated elite into a mass radical movement. (9)

Gilbert, Ben W. (ed.), *Ten Blocks from the White House* (a Praeger paperback). Reporters' accounts of the Washington riots following the assassination of Martin Luther King, Jr. (18)

Goode, Erich, ed., *Marijuana*. New York: Atherton Press, Inc., 1969. A collection of short readings on the reasons for taking the drug, its effects, if it leads to more powerful drugs, buying and selling drugs in the schools, legal questions. (20)

Kobrin, Solomon, "The Chicago Area Project—A 25-Year Assessment," *Annals of the American Academy of Political and Social Science*, Vol. 322 (March 1959), pp. 20–29. Believing that delinquency is the outcome of forces in the community, the Chicago Area Project attempted to reduce delinquency by organizing the local forces opposed to crime so that the neighborhood's influence would be *against* delinquency. (5, 6, 7, 8)

———, "Conflict of Values in Delinquency Areas," *American Sociological Review*, Vol. 16 (October 1951), pp. 653–661. In various areas of the city, legal and illegal systems of behavior exist together in varying proportions. Where population changes rapidly, the systems are not integrated and values are confused. Young persons growing up there may choose unacceptable careers. (6, 7)

———, "Sociological Aspects of the Development of a Street-Corner Group: An Explorative Study," *American Journal of Orthopsychiatry*, Vol. 31, No. 5 (October 1961), pp. 685–702. A gang of peers is often a boy's only avenue of social learning. A four-year study of a 16-member group shows how younger boys find places in the gang, while the older ones pass out of it; how their values change between childhood and adolescence. (5, 6, 7, 8)

Landesco, John, *Organized Crime in Chicago*. Chicago: University of Chicago Press, 1968. (Also a Phoenix paperback, 1968.) An account of the working of the "crime syndicate" in the twenties and early thirties, the lawless time of Prohibition and Al Capone. (10, 16)

Lang, Kurt, and Lang, Gladys Engel, "Racial Disturbances as Collective Protest," *The American Behavioral Scientist*, Vol. 11, No. 4 (March–April 1968), pp. 11–13. A review of rioting in the late 1960s presents: (1) riots as part of the civil rights movement; and (2) the deterrent to riots as the extension of full civil rights to blacks. (18)

Leinwand, Gerald, ed., *Crime and Juvenile Delinquency*. New York: Washington Square Press (paperback). Part I is a general discussion of problems of urban crimes and juvenile delinquency: What are the causes of crime and delinquency? Can crime and delinquency be prevented? Part II is a selection of dramatic readings. (4, 5, 6, 7, 8, 11, 12)

Lewis, Oscar, *La Vida: A Puerto Rican Family in the Culture of Poverty—San Juan and New York.* New York: Random House, Inc., 1966. (Also a Vintage paperback.)

Five households of the Ríos family, living in poverty and crime in the slums of New York and San Juan. (5, 6, 7, 15)

———, *A Study of Slum Culture: Backgrounds for La Vida.* New York: Random House, Inc., 1968.

A study of 50 Puerto Rican families in four slums—San Juan, Puerto Rico, and Manhattan, Brooklyn, and Bronx, New York—to discover the essential elements in "the culture of poverty." (5, 6, 7, 15)

Liebow, Elliot, *Tally's Corner: A Story of Negro Street Corner Men.* Boston: Little, Brown & Company, 1967 (paperback).

Description of the domestic and work lives and leisure activities of black unskilled workers, often unemployed. (5, 6, 7)

Loth, David G., *Crime in the Suburb.* New York: William Morrow & Company, 1967.

Relates crime in the city to poverty and physical deprivation but crime in the suburbs to abundance and excessive permissiveness that often leads to emotional deprivation. (6, 9, 11, 12, 15)

Matza, David, and Sykes, Gresham M., "Juvenile Delinquency and Subterranean Values," *American Sociological Review,* Vol. 26, No. 5 (October 1961), pp. 712–719.

Explains the attractiveness of delinquent behavior by comparing its gratifications with the gratifications of conforming behavior in moments of leisure and play. Thus delinquency can be expected in *all* youth, not just the disadvantaged. (2, 3)

Moore, William J., *The Vertical Ghetto: Everyday Life in an Urban Project.* New York: Random House, Inc., 1969.

Study of the daily lives of 100 Midwest families shows the ill effects on family life and on children of the crowded life in certain low-income public housing projects. (5, 6, 7)

Nowlis, Helen H., *Drugs on the Campus.* New York: Doubleday & Company, Inc., 1969.

Drugs classified; effects of each type; LSD and the "student culture"; the social influences on drug-taking; drugs and the law. (20)

O'Donnell, John A., "Narcotic Addiction and Crime," *Social Problems,* Vol. 13, No. 4 (Spring 1966), pp. 374–375.

A follow-up on Kentucky addicts. Most are criminals already, and then commit more crimes. Review and research. (20)

Parker, Tony, *Women in Crime*. New York: Delacorte Press, 1968. (Also a Delta paperback.)
Case studies of five girls who are juvenile delinquents. (5, 6, 7)

Sears, David O., and McConahay, John B., "Participation in the Los Angeles Riot," *Social Problems*, Vol. 17, No. 1 (Summer 1969), pp. 3–20.
A survey of the black community of Los Angeles reveals that rioters were not a small local minority, nor the less educated, the unemployed, or the recent migrants to the city; and that the rioting was generally regarded as a protest on the part of black youth. (18)

Shaw, Clifford R., and McKay, Henry D., *Juvenile Delinquency and Urban Areas*. Chicago: University of Chicago Press, 1942 and 1969.
The distribution of male juvenile delinquents in Chicago, 1927–1933; high- and low-rate communities, relation to other local problems: truancy, infant mortality, TB, mental disorder; difference in social values in the local communities; the same data for other cities. (4, 5, 6, 7, 11)

Short, James F., Jr., and Strodtbeck, Fred L., "Why Gangs Fight," *Trans-Action*, Vol. 1, No. 6 (September–October 1964), pp. 25–29.
In a conflict gang, status must be managed so that the gang and the members preserve their "rep." In a retreatist gang, "the trip" is the focus of interest. (5, 6, 7, 12, 20)

Smith, Thomas S., "Conventionalization and Control: An Examination of Adolescent Crowds," *The American Journal of Sociology*, LXXIV, No. 2 (September, 1968), pp. 172–183.
Observation over five years of Labor Day riots of teenagers at a beach resort, revealing how leaders of cliques make use of these occasions to increase their own status. Riots tend to follow a pattern and to become conventionalized. (9)

Sykes, Gresham M., *The Society of Captives: A Study of a Maximum Security Prison*. Princeton, N.J.: Princeton University Press, 1958. (Also an Atheneum paperback.)
Chapter IV describes the situations in prison which lead men into certain roles; Chapter V reports prison language ("rat," "squealer," etc.) expressing these roles. (13)

Toby, Jackson, "Hoodlum or Business Man: An American Dilemma," in Sklare, Marshall, ed., *The Jews*. New York: The Free Press, 1958, pp. 542–550.

Shows how fateful a boy's associations are in leading him to choose a "straight" or a criminal career, with comments on the case of Jewish boys. (6, 7, 8)

Wellford, Charles, "Factors Associated with the Adoption of the Inmate Code: A Study of Normative Socialization," *Journal of Criminal Law, Criminology, and Police Science,* Vol. 58, No. 2 (June 1967), pp. 197–203.

A study of a sample drawn from a prison population, 85 percent black, in the District of Columbia, revealed that personality and experiences *before* imprisonment affected an inmate's attitude to prison authorities. (6, 7, 13)

Whyte, William Foote, *Street Corner Society: The Social Structure of an Italian Slum.* Chicago: University of Chicago Press, 1943. (Also a Phoenix paperback, 1955.)

A study of a street gang of young Italian Americans in a slum in an eastern city and of the lives of its members; with analysis of what held them together, how one of them assumed leadership, their relations with other gangs and politics and racketeering. (5, 6, 7, 16, 17)

Wolfgang, Marvin E., "Who Kills Whom," *Psychology Today,* Vol. 3, No. 5 (October 1969), pp. 55–56, 72–75.

Generalizations from a five-year study of 588 homicides in Philadelphia; for example, two-thirds of victims are relatives or intimates of the murderer; one-fifth of victims are the husband or wife; the race line is rarely crossed, the sex line oftener, etc. (9)

Yablonsky, Lewis, *The Violent Gang.* New York: Macmillan and Company, 1962, pp. 143–152, 222–227. (Also a Pelican paperback.)

Gangs are classified and the circumstances under which they grow violent are discussed. (6, 7, 20)

INDEX

Page numbers in italics indicate the first page of a reading by the author.

Addiction (See Drugs)
Adolescence:
  changing requirements of, 84, 85
  in nineteenth-century America, 82
Aggravated assault, 137
Alcohol, 188, 191, 192, 193, 194
Alcoholics, 7, 8, 176, 178, 180, 182, 183–184, 187, 192, 193, 195
American Revolution, 170
"American way of life," 171
Amphetamines, 188, 193, 194
Anti-Catholic riots, 166
Anti-Chinese riots, 166
Antidepressants, 188
Anti-Negro riots, 166
Anti-war demonstrations, 7
Assault, 135, 137
Auto theft:
  and age of delinquent, 118
  cultural reasons for, 116
  and family background, 117–118
  as a "group crime," 119
  and intelligence of delinquent, 118
  percentage of grand larcenies committed, 113
  personal reasons for, among teen-age boys, 114–116
  as a white, middle-class crime, 116–117

Barbiturates, 188, 191, 192, 193
Betting (See Gambling; Organized crime)
Bingo (See Gambling)
Black Panthers, 62

Blum, Richard H., 7, 8, 186
Boston, in crime study, 1849–1951, 130–141
Bowery, 176, 184, 185
Briar, Scott, 4, 18
Burglary, 134, 137, 140

Capone, Al, 94, 152
Car theft (See Auto theft)
Caseríos, in San Juan, 147–148
Cavan, Ruth Shonle, 2, 5, 9
Chicago Area Projects, 122
Children's Bureau, 10
Civil War draft riots, 166
Class structure, in America, 80
Clinard, Marshall B., 3, 142
Cloward, Richard A., 5, 51
Columbia University, student occupation of, 168
Confessions of an English Opium Eater, The, 187
Constitution, 170
"Contracultures," 14, 17
Correctional agencies, effects on delinquents, 21
Corruption (See Graft and Corruption)
Cosa Nostra, 169
Crime:
  and the arrest rate, 137, 138
  and the automobile, 112–119, 131–132, 136, 139
  and changes in the social structure, 130, 136, 138, 139, 140–141
  and civil rights, 8
  and decay of the city, 141
  decline of, in Boston, 1875–1951, 131, 132
  defined, 2

Crime (*continued*)
and drug usage, 193–194
and ethnic minorities, 141
and immigration, 139
organized, 6–7, 54, 55, 56, 149–156, 157–164
and poverty, 6, 93, 99
rate in urban U.S., 130
and recidivism, 120–128
rising rate in Boston since 1951, 140–141
and the slums, 54–55, 141
and social class, 6
and the standard of living, 139
Sutherland on, 92–101
and urban growth, 139, 141, 144, 145, 146
and wars and depressions, 136, 137, 138
white-collar, 6, 91–101
"Crime index," 130

Davidson County, Tenn., study of delinquency in, 73
Delinquency (See Juvenile delinquency)
Delirium tremens, 188
Democratic National Convention of 1968, 168
Dentler, Robert A., 6, *102*
Department of Motor Vehicles of the State of New York, 149
Depressants, 193
Depression, 166, 177, 185
"Deprivation theory," of gang behavior, 47, 50
De Quincey, Thomas, 187
"Deviance," 2
Discrimination, by police, 24–26
Disorderly conduct, 2
Draft, conflict over, 169
"Drag racing," 87, 88
Drugs:
and automobile accidents, 193
classification of, 188
and criminal behavior, 193–194

dangers of, 191–193
dependency on, 190
and drug addiction, 7, 190, 193, 194
and drug-influenced behavior, 188–189
and ghetto males, 195
in high school, 80–81
history of, 187
increased usage of, 187
and organized crime, 152, 153, 154, 156
reasons for using, 189–191
in the slums, 58–59
social use of, 191
and the treatment of drug-takers, 195
"Drunks on Skid Row, 180–182, 183

Embezzlement, 97
Empey, LaMar T., 4, 27
'Erickson, Maynard L., 4, 27
"Establishment," 169, 172
Euphoriants, 188
Expense account padding, 100
Extended family, among Poles and Italians, 124, 127

Family, changing patterns of the, 83–84
Federal Bureau of Investigation (FBI), 1, 97, 113, 140, 160, 162
Federal Trade Commission, 96
Fee-splitting, among doctors, 94
Ferdinand, Theodore N., 3, 8, *129*
Finestone, Harold, 7, *120*
Food and Drug Administration, 96

Gambling:
in Britain, 164
hidden nature of, 162
legalized forms of, 159
in Nevada, 164

and organized crime, 152, 154, 156, 159
public attitudes toward, 158, 160, 163–164
in the slums, 66, 67
Gangs, delinquent:
activities of, 44–45, 52–53, 69
and adolescent alienation, 50
"deprivation theory" of, 47, 50
and importance of "belonging," 188
and masculinity, 49
occupations of members of, 48
peer loyalty of 49
socioeconomic background of, 45–47, 54
and status, 5, 68–69, 70
"wars" of, 70
and the youth culture, 5, 47, 49
Gardiner, John A., 6–7, 157
General Motors, 92
Graft and corruption:
political, 158
public attitudes toward, 161–162, 164
as a white-collar crime, 97
Greeley, Horace, 186

Hallucinogens, 188, 194
Harvard, building seizure at, 169
Hashish, 187
Heroin, 188, 190, 192, 193, 194
High schools:
and the growth of peer groups, 85–86
permissive character of, 85
"socializing" function of, 85
Hippies, 187
Hobos, 182, 184
Human behavior:
nonconforming, 10
overconforming, 10, 12, 13
range of, 10–11, 15, 17
and social class, 16
underconforming, 10, 12, 13

Human nature, beliefs of Poles and Italians about, 127–128
Illegal driving, correlated with theft among teenagers, 109, 110, 111
Illinois State Penitentiary System, 122
Imprisonment, system of, 7
Internal Revenue Service, 160
Intoxicants, 188
IWW (International Workers of the World), 182

Johnson, Earl, Jr., 6, 149
Joy riding, 81, 87, 88
Justice Department, United States, 130, 163
Juvenile Bureau, duties of, 20, 21
Juvenile delinquency:
amount of, 30–33
and cars, 88
conformity as cause of, 87
and the cult of masculinity, 89
definitions of, 2, 9–10
as a function of opportunity, 89–90
and lower-class culture, 62–71
among middle-class youth, 8, 80–90
most common types of, 34
prolonged adolescence as cause of, 82–83
rate of, for boys, by delinquency rate of residential area, in Tennessee study, 76–78
rate of, for boys, by father's occupation and school's status, in Tennessee study, 74–76
role of police and courts in labeling, 73
and sex, 88–89
and social class, 16–17, 39–42
and status, 34, 72–79, 87
"status frustration" theory of, 77–78

Juvenile delinquency (*continued*)
    undetected, 28, 34, 35, 38–39,
        42
Juvenile offenders:
    frequency of offenses commit-
        ted by, 35
    noninstitutionalized compared
        with institutionalized, 38
    one-time offenders contrasted
        with persistent, 38
    proportions of, committing cer-
        tain offenses, 36–37
    reliability of court records on,
        38
    serious offenses committed by,
        35

Kansas study, of teen-age thieves,
    103–111
Karacki, Larry, 5, *43*
King, Martin Luther, Jr., 168, 172

Larceny, 135, 138
"Law and order," 1
Law enforcement:
    discrimination in, 4
    in Wincanton, 160
Leary, Timothy, 186–187
Limited democracy, 170
Lotteries (See Gambling; Organ-
    ized Crime)
LSD, 187, 188, 190, 192
Lynchings, 166

"Machismo," 190
Mafia, 56, 151, 154
Manslaughter, 131, 133, 136
Marijuana, 60, 187, 188, 190,
    193, 194
Middle class:
    juvenile delinquency in, 80–90
    and the Protestant ethic, 83
    social and economic changes
        affecting, 84
    traditional values of, 82–84
    transformation of family struc-
        ture in, 84
Miller, Walter B., 5, 8, *62*

Monroe, Lawrence J., 6, *102*
Mormons, in study of undetected
    delinquency, 28, 42
Morphine, 188, 191, 192
Murder, 2, 131, 132

Narcotics, 188
Narcotics traffic, 152, 156
Nation, Carrie, 14
National Crime Commission, 163
National Guard, 168
Nativists, 171–173, 174
New York Training School for
    Boys (See Warwick)
Nuclear family, in Polish-Ameri-
    can culture, 124, 127
Numbers rackets (See Gambling;
    Organized crime)
Nye, F. Ivan, 17, 104

Ohlin, Lloyd E., 5, *51*
Opium, 187
Organized crime:
    and athletics, 154
    business structure of, 6–7, 54
    connections needed by, 55
    and drugs, 153, 154
    economic costs of, 152
    and gambling, 152, 154, 156,
        159
    murders and maimings by,
        152–153
    and official corruption, 154–
        155, 158, 161–162, 163,
        164
    and prostitution, 152
    and public indifference to, 156
    and the reform movement, 158,
        163
    and the undermining of social
        morality, 155
    and vice, 153
    in Wincanton, 157–164
Organized Crime and Racketeer-
    ing Section of the United
    States Department of Jus-
    tice, 151

Peer group:
conformism in, 85, 86–87
functions of, for adolescents, 86
origins of, 85–86
Pendergast, "Boss" (Thomas Joseph), 97
"Pep pills," 187
Peyote, 187
Piliavin, Irving, 4, *18*
Police discretion, and juveniles, 21–26
Police violence, 168–169, 172–173
"Pot," 81, 190
Powers, John Arthur, 153
President's Commission on Civil Disorders, 167–168
President's Committee on Law Enforcement and the Administration of Justice, 188
Price-fixing, 92, 95
Prostitution, 147, 152
"Protestant ethic," 83, 84
Public Accommodations Section, of civil rights law, 167
Puerto Rico:
drug addiction in, 143
juvenile delinquency in, 143
modernization of, 142–143
urbanization of, 143
Pullman Strike, 166

Racketeering, 152
Rape, 133, 136–137
Recidivism:
defined, 122
and drinking, 124–125
and employment, 125–126
and environment of released criminal, 122, 128
and marital status, 123–124
and peer group influences, 126–127
and pressures toward criminality, 126

rate, among Italians and Poles, 123
Reconstructivists, 171–173, 174
Registry of Motor Vehicles, in New York, 150
Rehabilitation, of criminals, 121–122, 123, 125, 127, 128
Reiss, Albert J., Jr., 6, *72*
Reserve Officers Training Corps, 174
Retreatism, 58, 61
Rhodes, Albert Lewis, 6, *72*
Riots (See Violence)
"Robber barons," 93
Robbery, 134, 137, 140
Rockefeller, (Nelson), 193
Rubington, Earl, 8, *175*

San Juan:
crime in, 146–148
population of, 143
prostitution in, 147
public housing in, 147–148
slums of, 146–148
Schepses, Erwin, 6, *112*
Scott, Joseph W., 6, 8, *80*
Securities and Exchange Commission, 96
Sedatives, 188
Sellin, Thorsten, 1
Shay's Rebellion, 165
Short, James F., Jr., 17, 104
"Shylocking," 152
Simple assault, 137
Skid Row:
alcoholics in, 176, 178, 180, 182, 183–184
beggars in, 183, 184
decline of, 184, 185
dislocation of inhabitants of, 177
"drunks" of, 180–182, 183
exposure to life of, 178
hierarchy of, 179–184
hobos of, 182, 184
integration of inhabitants of, 179

Skid Row (*continued*)
  misconceptions about, 176
  "mission stiffs" and "reliefers" in, 183, 184
  participation in activities of, 179
  as part of American urban life, 175–176
  "tour directors" of, 183, 184
Slums:
  alcoholism and drug addiction in, 58
  attitude toward autonomy in, 67
  attitude toward fate in, 66–67
  attitudes toward "smartness" in, 65–66
  attitudes toward "toughness" in, 65
  attitudes toward "trouble" in, 64
  and delinquency, 5, 6, 8
  and "excitement," 66
  and female-dominated households, 64, 65, 68
  gambling in, 66, 67
  "integrated," 55
  marital patterns in, 64
  of San Juan, 146–148
  as training ground for criminals, 54–55
  "unintegrated," 55–58
  values of, 70–71
Social status, and delinquency, 73–79
Spanish-American War, 142
"Speed," 187, 193
Spiegel, John P., 7, *165*
"Status frustration," theory of, 77–78, 79
Stealing, among teen-agers in Kansas study, 103–111
Stern, Irv, 159, *163*
Stickney, A. B., 93
Stimulants, 188
Stolen-car racket, 149–151
Student disturbances, 7, 174

"Subsistence economy," 144
Sutherland, Edwin H., 6, *91*

Teen-age culture (See Youth culture)
Teen-age drinking, 80–81, 88, 90
Theft (See Larceny; Stealing; Thieves)
Thieves, teen-age:
  and church attendance, 108
  leisure-time activities of, 108–109
  number of, 104
  and other forms of delinquency, 109–111
  and relations with parents, 106–107
  and self-esteem, 111
  social and personal characteristics of, 103, 104–106, 108
  and working mothers, 107–108
Toby, Jackson, 5, *43*
Tranquilizers, 188, 192

Upward mobility, in America, 83, 84
Urbanization:
  and crime rate, 144, 145, 146
  effects on rural migrants, 144–146
  of U.S. population, 130

Vandalism, correlated with theft among teen-agers, 109, 110, 111
Vanderbilt, Commodore (Cornelius), 93
Vaz, Edmund W., 6, 8, *80*
Violence:
  basic causes of, 169–170
  of blacks against whites, 167–168
  collective, 167, 169
  contradictions between American ideals and practice as cause of, 170–171, 174
  cycle of, 165–166, 174

defined, 166
against people, 168, 172
of police against demonstrators, 7, 168–169, 172–173
against property, 168, 172
shared power as means of ending, 174
of whites against blacks, 167

Wallace, George, 173
Wallace, Samuel E., 8, 175
Warwick, study of teen-age auto thieves in, 113–119
Watts, riot in, 170
Welfare, protests over, 168, 174
West Point, United States Military Academy at, 91
West Side Story, 62
White-collar crime:
  compared with lower-class crime, 98–99
  cost of, 95–96
  extent of, 94–95
  lenient treatment of, 98

proposed definition of, 96–97
Sutherland on, 92–101
types of, 94
victims of, 98
Wincanton, organized crime in, 157–164
"Withdrawal sickness," 190
Women's rights, 173–174
Working class, attitudes toward protesters, 173

Youth culture:
  activities of, 87
  and the American economy, 84
  and automobiles, 88
  and dating behavior, 88–89
  and drinking, 80–81, 88, 90
  and drugs, 187
  and the educational system, 85
  as explanation for gangs, 5, 47, 49
  and the family system, 83–84
  and peer groups, 85–86
  rise, 82

American Sociological Association
Advisory Committee

Sociological Resources
for the Social Studies